Beliefs and How to Change Them

A manual of methods for changing beliefs in ourselves and others

By Larry Westenberg

Published by Expanding Enterprises, Inc.
www.expandingenterprises.com

IMPORTANT NOTE:

This book is NOT intended to teach you all about how to change beliefs. If everything involved in changing beliefs could be explained in 200 or so pages, many people would have already taught how to do this in many other books. This book is an introduction to the tools and techniques used to change beliefs utilizing different models from advanced Neuro-Linguistic Programming or NLP training.

Visit: www.expandingenterprises.com for the training programs required to make this information work most effectively!

If you are interested in getting these pieces to fit together to accomplish correctly changing beliefs, you would need to attend several training programs offered by Expanding Enterprises, Inc., the company that teaches all of the information not included in these manual excerpts. Expanding Enterprises, Inc. offers training in "Human Animal Behavior Trainingsm" or HABTsm. HABTsm training goes far beyond NLP training standards, and its focus is on what technique to use when, based on the client's presentation. (Most NLP graduates have a terrible time trying to figure out what technique to use for which problem.) It also incorporates a variety of methods from neuro-psychology, cognitive therapy, mindfulness, Gestalt therapy and The Radiance Technique®. These techniques combine into a holistic change process that not only shifts problems and symptoms, but also opens up gateways to discover new levels of your own being. We offer classes that teach NLP models and techniques in a specific context. We offer classes such as, "Learning to Enjoy Life More," and, "Resolving Conflicts – Inside and Out."

If you have Master Practitioner Certification in Neuro-Linguistic Programming from a good training institute, you should be able to utilize the steps and methods offered in this book to complete the given steps and techniques. As you have already (hopefully) learned, please be careful and ecological in making changes at the very powerful and potentially generative level of beliefs. Even subtle little changes in wordings have tremendous impact. For example, while playing with changing my own beliefs, I once changed my belief about myself to, "I can do anything." In this spirit, I emphatically set off to go to the store to start some projects! I climbed into my car, backed out of the driveway, and put the car in gear to begin my quest to take over the earth. I suddenly froze. For the first time in my life, I had just backed my car out of my driveway and onto a street without looking for traffic. I suddenly realized (after a very hard swallow from the fear about what I had just done) that the more accurate and precise belief I needed to accomplish my mission was, "I can LEARN any information I want to learn." I had decided I wanted to go to graduate school, and I wanted to install in myself a belief that would help me. It was just a little too general - and it almost killed me. Be careful.

Larry Westenberg
2018

Table of Contents

Introduction 1
  Why Write a Book on Changing Beliefs? 3
  Acknowledgements 3

Section 1: Overview 7
  Overview of the Book 9

Section 2: Foundations of Neuro-Linguistic Programming (NLP) - Anchoring 11
  Anchoring 13
    Practice Exercise – Pillar of Excellence 16
    Practicing 17
      Where Can I Use this Information? 17
  Anchoring-Based NLP Techniques 18
    Practice Exercises 18
      Anchoring Disassociation Exercise 19
    Common Indicators of Disassociation 19
      Chaining From a Stuck State to Disassociation Exercise 20
    Anchoring Resources to New Contexts Exercises 20
      Behavioral Context Transfer Exercise 20
      Borrowing New Behaviors Exercise 21
    Anchoring to Add Past and Future Resources 22
      Change Personal History Exercise 22

Section 3: Beliefs 25
  Why Do People Build Beliefs? 26
    Why Intentionally Build Beliefs? 26
    Thinking about Thinking 27
  Beliefs Get "Paired" with States 28
  The Three Sources of Beliefs 29
  The Structure of Beliefs 31
    What is a Frame? 31
    An Example of Frames: 32
    Another Example of Frames 33
    Mr. Smith and the Cellular Store 33
    Mrs. Jones and Her Failed Life 35
  Levels of Abstraction 37
    The Evidence for Evidence 40
  Values 43
    Beliefs and Values 46
    Values and Meaning 46
  Logical Levels 49
    Beliefs are Recursive Evaluations 52

Beliefs Lead to States 53
   The 4th Component of a Belief 53
The Two Types of Beliefs 55

Section 4: Structures for Belief Systems 57

Beliefs and Time 59
   The "In-Time Person" 59
   The "Through-Time Person" 59
   The "Between-Time Person" 59
The Three Types of Belief Structures 60
Frames, Chunk Size and Scope 61

Section 5: Changing Beliefs Using NLP Models 67

Changing Beliefs Using NLP Models 69
   Honesty and Ethics 69
   Well-Formedness Conditions for Beliefs 70
   Believing and States 71
Changing Beliefs Using Sequenced Anchoring 72
   Anchoring-Based NLP Techniques 73
   Component States to Anchor for Belief Change 73
   Changing Beliefs by Sequenced Anchors 75
   Instructions: Changing Beliefs by Sequenced Anchors - Script 76
Changing Beliefs Using Sub-Modalities 79
   Overview 80
Changing Beliefs Using Strategies 82
   Overview 82
One More Distinction about Evidence and Convincing 86

Section 4: Changing Beliefs with Language and NLP Models 89

Weakening Beliefs with NLP Models 91
   Weakening Beliefs with States 91
   Weakening Beliefs with Submodalities 91
Changing Beliefs with Language 92
   Part 1: Weakening Beliefs – "Sleight-of-Mouth" 92
   Part 2: Strengthening Beliefs – Presuppositions 92
The Four Categories of SOM Patterns 95
   Time SOM Patterns 98
   Existence SOM Patterns 102
   Quality SOM Patterns 107
   Meaning SOM Patterns 112
Presuppositions – Opposite of SOM 117
   What Is a Presupposition? 118
   Examples of Presuppositions Exercise 119
How do Presuppositions Work? 120
The 3 Categories of Presuppositional Forms 124
   A Word about Practice 125
A Little Test… 151
   Wrapping It All Together 155

Section 5: Beliefs That Could Change the World 157

Beliefs That Could Change the World 159

Three Beliefs that Could Destroy the World: 159

Three Beliefs that Could Save the World: 162

An Amazing Fact about Cooperation 164

Section 6: Changing Generalizations About People and Groups 165

Changing Generalizations about People and Groups 167

Creating Positive People Beliefs...168

How to Teach and Practice Tolerance...168

Section 7: Final Thoughts on How to Identify "Good" Beliefs 171

Final Thoughts on How to Identify "Good" Beliefs 173

Version 5.1

Introduction

Why Write a Book on Changing Beliefs?

Long ago, I began studying something called Neuro-Linguistic Programming or NLP. NLP made some pretty incredible claims about what it could do. One of the claims that most fascinated me was that NLP could influence people's limiting beliefs. I first learned to do this at a very small scale, and practiced my skills by working in sales. I convinced people they needed to buy something. I kept my integrity – I never sold people things they didn't want or need. It became frighteningly easy to sell people things, and I resigned because I knew too much about influencing people's buying beliefs. Besides – I had bigger fish to fry! In those days, I worked full-time with the criminally insane in a large state mental health center. It was one thing to be able to convince a housewife to buy a telephone answering machine. But I wanted to be able to convince someone who thought it was "cool" to kill people that it was actually BAD to kill people. THAT is why I learned this stuff. I practiced and practiced, and I got pretty good at it. However, while many of my patients changed and got better/stable, I never did quite master the art of convincing a judge I never saw or talked to that the client was now stable and ready to be discharged. So the patient's got better, but it didn't help them at all. They were still in the hospital. I left to move on to bigger and better things.

I most certainly did not learn these techniques overnight. I worked hard, practiced, experimented, screwed-up, got lucky, cried in frustration, gave-up a few times, got back into it, persisted, and finally I decided this was incredibly useful material for the world.

I became absolutely convinced that the world needed to learn techniques for understanding and changing harmful beliefs in themselves and others on September 11th, 2001. On that date, I witnessed the impact of some people who actually believed that driving airplanes into buildings full of civilians was in some way a good thing to do. I cried a lot. I felt shocked that there could be that much hate, prejudice, and intentional hurt in the world. Then I decided to finish this book, in hopes that it would help change things for the better.

Acknowledgements

I am forever indebted to Mr. Charles Faulkner for the notion of all beliefs having the metaphoric structure of containers. It was this unique filter that helped me to notice relationships in patterns and linguistic sequences in NLP I had never noticed previously. It also helped me notice relationships in language patterns that I don't believe anyone else has documented.

I have had the privilege of many good teachers. I got to wherever I am with a lot of support from other people in many different forms. One of my most powerful mentors was my college music professor, Dean Karns. Dean was the most polite and graceful negotiator, and I was a bulldozer. I watched him pull off incredible negotiations, and figured I should attempt to adopt his smooth style. I never was able to do that. Dean introduced me to The

Radiance Technique® in 1986, for which I am forever grateful – as I was very skeptical. We have kept in touch through conferences for The Radiance Technique®, and are still friends.

Some other powerful influences that have helped me survive have been George Mohn, David Brown, Melodie Fox, Barbara Aurora, Matt and Claire Gronwald, Michael Young, Dr. Barbara Ray, and Dr. Barbara Ray. Yes, that was on purpose. I do not think I would have survived until the age of 30 without the support of The Radiance Technique®. Also Mr. Richard Bahwell from Coe College for noticing and encouraging my rabid excitement at learning, and Shoshanna Shay for her loving heart. I also want to thank my junior high school orchestra teacher Mrs. Sue Kuriga-Thorne, for helping me believe my life would get better if I just hung in there. I have also been beautifully helped in integrating NLP by John-Michael McClean, and Joe Winterseik. When it was time for deeply changing my own brain programs, these are the gentlemen I trusted to do that.

I want to both deeply thank and humorously curse at Coe College in Cedar Rapids, Iowa. I want to thank them for an incredibly challenging, intensive and open-minded education. I was taught and encouraged to ask questions, think for myself, draw my own conclusions and defend them. I want to curse Coe College for somehow leaving me with the impression that these skills would be valued in graduate school. They were not. Graduate school seemed to me to be about being a good little sheep and agreeing with the teacher's perspective, echoing the party line and not experimenting. Deep gratitude also to The Lucis Trust and their Arcane School, which has challenged me incredibly throughout my entire life (lucistrust.org).

When I began studying NLP in 1989, I felt like I had discovered what I had been looking for all of my life. Here was a way to help people change that was quick, subtle, and extremely powerful. I felt the same way when I studied The Radiance Technique® for the first time in 1986. Later I discovered that both NLP and TRT® can be applied in a million different ways.

I studied NLP with many students of Richard Bandler. His signature is on all of my certificates, however, I did not study very much directly from him. I did have the honor of being in the audience at two DHE™ trainings and two "weekends" he did. And yes, DHE™ changed my life. I think "all them lights and strategies and stuff" helped me get through graduate school, and helped me create a system called "Human Animal Behavior Trainingsm" (HABTsm) that I am currently teaching. This system offers a person trained in NLP techniques a way to know "which technique to use when" (the most common NLP graduate question!) in a simple and logical way that is not taught in any NLP training. It also teaches how to combine multiple interventions into powerful packages for change.

If Richard Bandler is the "male" side of NLP, I have had the privilege of studying with a "Power Trio" of women in NLP as well. That would be Connirae Andreas, Ph.D., Lindagail Campbell, and Laura Ewing. Each of them lives their incredible congruence in a different way, and each of them is a model for living in congruence. They are the kind of people who help you change just by standing close to you. I'm not kidding at all. Dr. Barbara Ray is like that also, and she uses a totally different technique.

4

I have also studied NLP with Charles Faulkner, Gerry Schmidt, Robert McDonald, Tamara Andreas, Steve Andreas, Rex Sikes, Tim Halbom, Suzi Smith, and others. I worked with Dr. Michael Banks in Chicago, whose "Conversational Change" classes and practice groups helped me integrate NLP into my own clinical style. And my mother taught me content reframing before I ever knew it was "called something."

I learned the most NLP, as well as the most about NLP, from Charles Faulkner. However, I am convinced that my friend Charles is from another planet, because his brain is frighteningly incredible. His deep work in metaphors and his ability to explain and apply NLP models is beyond compare. He is a delightful genius and friend.

Throughout my studies of NLP, there has been a battle over who can certify, and who can say someone has studied, and what "is" NLP... I only offer this perspective. When I first saw Richard Bandler working with a client, that was what I wanted to learn, emulate and do. Let me be more specific - his "natural" and casual style, the caring and kind attitude of his early years - that was what I wanted to learn and emulate. Well, since we can all presuppose there is a positive intention behind every behavior, let's assume one positive intention of maintaining control of certification is to be able to maintain quality control, content control, and the ability to have some credence behind what it means to say, "I studied something called NLP." As a professional designer of training programs with a Master's degree in training design, this is exactly what I have been forced to do from the start with the training programs I create. It takes an immense amount of work to maintain the quality of training programs that are offered, license who can offer them, and control what materials are used when they do.

If you are going to "get into" NLP at all, you will soon realize that it is a "big field." You may want to get a handle on it from a lot of different perspectives. I highly recommend NLP training, and I recommend you explore different training institutes. Each appeals to different applications, and to different types of people. Each teaches different stuff, and calls it NLP training, though there is often a "core curriculum." You decide where and with whom you want to study. My own training institute specializes in teaching non-therapists to work with trauma and motivation. I also teach social workers, counselors, educators, nurses and other types of therapists. Our focus is on belief work. This ties in nicely with NLP and health, and a wide variety of other applications.

In another perspective, if the institute from which you are studying does not know how the pieces fit together to make NLP interventions work properly, then you get training you cannot use and apply in the real world. My goal is simply to be able to use and carefully teach NLP and other models, and make them work smoothly and easily so we can all learn to make people's lives more enjoyable and reduce suffering in the world.

One more perspective – NLP exists as a set of models, a set of perspectives. It exists on the mental plane. While there has to be a structure in mental processes, I do not think such mental processes need to be so closely regulated after a while. Any sufficiently large system begins to develop its own intelligence (according to Bateson), and I think that has happened within the field of NLP. It has taken off and grown on its own. However, NLP is based on a series of multi-level mental processes. I work with another technique to facilitate growth and change called "The Radiance Technique®." With The Radiance Technique®, the entire system MUST be intact, or the resulting "output" is not the same. The Radiance Technique® is the original intact system that was taught as "reiki" by Mrs. Hawayo Takata. It is now available under the protected and service marked name, "The Radiance Technique®. Anything now called "reiki" in NOT what Mrs. Takata taught, although they will attempt to define their "lineage" and otherwise convince you – or claim TRT® is a scam, or that it is "the same thing, just more expensive." This is misinformation based on misinformation they received. The intact system has seven degrees, not three. That is an enormous difference!

The difference is because genuine TRT® is an intact energy-based system. With NLP - I believe you can "get similar enough" to something that exists on the mental plane to get the same results.

The categorizations of language patterns discussed in this book were my own discovery, and the categorizations of how to apply them to beliefs are also mine. These distinctions were never "shown" to me by anyone. They were the result of working with the language patterns I got from Connirae Andreas' books and tapes, and my noticing that certain patterns worked on certain "kinds" of people. I sat and studied the presuppositional forms for four years as I got my Master's degrees. I began to get intimately "into" the different presuppositions, and thanks to my own sensory synesthesia, combined with skills I learned in Design Human Engineering™, I was able to detect patterns in my own thinking and make them explicit. The result is a totally new way to learn language patterns that I hope is helpful to people trying to master belief-changing skills. I applied these principles to both presuppositional forms, and the category of language patterns known as Sleight-of-Mouth. Check it out. I hope you like it!

Before I finish, I wish to thank Dr. Barbara Ray, for protecting The Intact Master Keys of The Radiance Technique®, assuring that the intact science would be available for me so I could have the incredible honor of studying to The Seventh Degree and working with TRT® in my life. I would have never made it through the stress of going to school while working full-time, nor been able to think through this insanely complex stuff without TRT® there at all times to support me. Check out www.trtia.org for more information on TRT® and The Radiance Technique International Association. Or, go to www.expandingenterprises.com to find out about how you can get training in The First Degree Official Program of The Radiance Technique® and The Second Degree Official Program of The Radiance Technique® from myself, as I am an Authorized Instructor of both of these training programs.

I also want to thank Neil Walker for making incredibly useful comments to the first drafts of this book. He challenged and questioned me with great skill, and if this book makes sense and is useful, it is largely because of his careful challenges.

And most of all, I hope you just plain enjoy this book!
Larry Westenberg - 2018

The Radiance Technique®, TRT®, The First Degree Official Program of The Radiance Technique®, The Second Degree Official Program of The Radiance Technique®, and The Intact Master Keys of The Radiance Technique® are all registered service marks held by The Radiance Technique International Association, Inc., and are used under license. (www.trtia.org)

Section 1: Overview

Overview of the Book

Have you ever noticed that people believe strange things? Having worked with the severely mentally ill, I have met people with some of the most bizarre beliefs in the world. Let me tell you about some bizarre beliefs, and use your imagination to "try them on." Please also be sure to "take them off" after your experiment!

I met a person who believed if a certain pattern of letters and numbers occurred in a license plate ahead of them, then God was giving them a special message telling them to kill the driver of that car. Now imagine if you believed that, and your best friend was borrowing a friend's car that just happened to have the fateful pattern. What would you do?

I met other people who believed the government was following them and trying to kill them, and they would look around the room and "find" microphones and bugs. I knew it was a thermostat – but they knew with equal certainty it was a microphone. Everybody has at least "moments of paranoia" when they think people are talking about them, or are planning something. It is a MOST unpleasant feeling – especially if it persists!

I met people who thought their mind was being read by other people, and they would line a hat with aluminum foil to interfere with the "brain waves" they believed they were transmitting. Now imagine if you believed this, and someone in the hospital came up to you and said they wanted to take an EEG! (An electronic measurement of the activity of your brain.)

I also met people who thought having the skin on their back split open with a sword or bullwhip was the most sexually exciting thing in the world. And they weren't patients in any mental health facility. Nor were the people who thought that the government was going to take away all of their civil rights and they needed to buy and store as many guns and weapons as possible because the government was going to come to their house to take away those civil rights. In fact, all of those people were employees of that mental health facility!

Have you ever been around people who had completely different beliefs than your own for any length of time? People's beliefs have a profound impact on their behavior. If you believe that you are part of a chosen group that is most certainly going to heaven because of specific things you believe, you don't have to be nice to anyone or put up with their lack of thinking like you. In fact, some groups use this as a reason to kill people who don't think the way they do. And that has been going on for thousands of years. Or, maybe you believe you have to be good to people and nice to them in order to get into heaven. Or maybe you don't believe in heaven at all.

As you learn about "Beliefs and How to Change Them," you can learn to influence people's beliefs, and even learn how to change them. I ask that you keep in mind two very important guidelines: **"Good beliefs" are beliefs that get people to treat other people with loving kindness and caring, or at least do no harm. Bad beliefs are beliefs that get people to treat others with hatred, hurt, or cold indifference.** Beliefs that enhance separateness are indeed a tremendous challenge to the world. I have no interest in helping people decide on any "truths." If that is why you got this book, you may as well attempt to return it. If you think you are going to change people's beliefs to agree with your own, I hope you will read this book and learn why that is absolutely unnecessary. But when you see people using their beliefs as a reason or excuse to treat other people badly, I hope you will use the skills and methods in this book to help them change and shift those beliefs. That way, we can all work together to make the world a nicer place to live for everyone who lives here on the planet.

IMPORTANT NOTE:

This book is NOT intended to teach you all about how to change beliefs. It is an introduction to the tools and techniques used to change beliefs. If you are interested in getting all of these pieces to fit together to smoothly accomplish changes, you will **need to attend training programs offered by Expanding Enterprises, Inc.**, the only company that teaches all of the information that is missing from these manual excerpts.

Visit: **www.expandingenterprises.com for more information**

Section 2:
Foundations of Neuro-Linguistic Programming (NLP) - Anchoring

Anchoring

Note: I argued about putting this chapter into the book, because of all people reading this book, the therapists will be the ones who think they can "think their way" through how to do anchoring – and won't practice it. They may even memorize the steps. But until a person actually and successfully anchors themselves AND other people, they will probably not benefit from just reading about HOW to anchor. Anchoring is the fundamental skill in NLP, and it is the most easy to learn – yet the most difficult to teach in a book. Go and participate in a training, because we want to make certain you pepper enjoyment and happiness into ALL of your anchors – and that is difficult to teach in a book!

The short version (1-day) of this training program is called, "Learning to Enjoy Life More." That is what it teaches. How to do exactly that. The certification version of this training program is two-days long and is called, "Natural Emotional Control Techniques," It teaches a huge number of additional practical anchoring methods.

If you wish to gain the most benefit, you need to PRACTICE anchoring with a group of people. Good storytellers are anchoring their audience through the ENTIRE story. Looking around, gesturing, using scary voices, small voices, shaky voices – all induce a state in the listener. So do the topics chosen. If you use them strategically, you can gain incredible impact. Anchor (pair specific states) with movements, with facial expressions you make, with voice tones, with touch – and most of all – anchor yourself so that you can have multiple powerful resource states available to you in the contexts and situations where you need them.

Much of what determines how much you enjoy life is how often you create or arrive at a resourceful state of being. This section is a gift to help you enjoy your job and your life more. However, you will need to practice and use the skill to develop it further. Fortunately, it is both simple to master, and has lots of payoff when you do it.

It is possible to have influence over the states of being you and others have throughout your entire life. In fact, you already have control of those states, although possibly not yet at a conscious level.

Have you ever known someone who could always put you in a good mood? Our interactions can help us guide people's attention, and this shifting can be directed to help us create a positive impact on people.

One of the quickest ways to do this is to pace or match a person's state, and then gradually "lead" by shifting your own state into a more positive state. In order to learn to do this really well, you need to first learn two distinct skills:
1. The ability to control and deliberately change your state both gradually and very quickly. We will show you and tell you how to do this.

2. To create and "develop" your own positive states. You need to learn how to experience more intense and more powerful positive states, and then "tailor" them to your needs. Being in "the right state for the situation" can help you accomplish more, and help you be happier.

As we mentioned, the exercises to learn these skills are a lot of fun to learn and practice. They should be done "externally" with a partner at first, but you can practice changing your state at any time, in any place, and completely internally. Learning to maintain your state has benefits far beyond what you can imagine.

You are about to enter a wonderful new world called, "Anchoring."

Basic Anchoring

Anchoring takes place when we deliberately put a "distinct cue" in place just prior to the peak of any "feeling wave." (See graph below)

Anchoring can be diagrammed as follows:

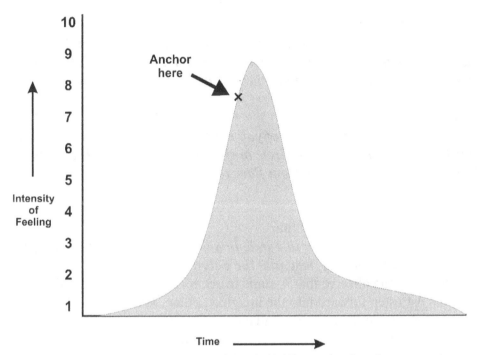

Notice that the cue (called the anchor) is deliberately timed to occur **just prior to the peak** of the feeling.

Now that we have started using the word, let us explain something about anchors and anchoring.

The process of pairing an "outer" stimulus with an internal state was discovered long ago by Ivan Pavlov in 1927. In approximately 1984, this phenomenon was capitalized upon by Richard Bandler and John Grinder in the early days of Neuro-Linguistic Programming, and doing this pairing process was called, "Anchoring." Anchoring is Pavlovian conditioning.

The specific and distinct "cue event" is referred to as "an anchor." In the early days of NLP when someone had a very positive state happen, someone else would say, "Anchor that!" Not only is anchoring very useful, the process called anchoring is used by some of the most powerful speakers and salespeople in the world to give greater impact to their communication.

Practice Exercise – Pillar of Excellence

(In trios – A, B and C. Rotate after 10 minutes)
Adapted from the original "Circle of Excellence" exercise, this exercise teaches you how to experience states of being you want to have more often in life. (Gratitude to Tom Grinder for teaching this technique via pillars.)

1. **Identify Excellent State**
   "What state of excellence would you like to have more places in your life?"
   "By a 'state of excellence', I mean a state in which you have lots of resources available to you. You may call it feeling 'jazzed' or confident or excited."

2. **Set up Pillar of Excellence**
   "I'd like you to imagine, right in front of you a pillar of excellence on the floor. What color is yours? Now allow the circle to rise up from the floor, becoming a pillar of color right in front of you, from floor to ceiling. Does it sing, buzz or hum?"

3. **Access Excellence and Anchor to Pillar**
   "Think of a time when you were in this state in a way that was very satisfying to you. As you begin to feel it fully, step into the pillar."
   a.) As soon as B can observe that A starts to access an excellent state, B motions A to step forward into the imagined pillar. B makes sure that a powerful state is fully accessed, and calibrates to this state. (i.e., memorizes what they look like in this state, how they breathe in this state, the sound of their voice in this state, etc.)

4. **Separator State**
   "Now step back out of the pillar."
   a.) Distract and change A's state with a neutral question that is totally out of context) *"What is your phone number backwards?"* *"What was the color of the front door of the house you grew up in?"*

5. **Repeat steps 2 through 4 twice more. Repeat all of the scripted verbal instructions above.**

6. **Testing**
   "Now step back into the pillar, and find out how fully it elicits those positive feelings."
   a.) B makes sure that A re-accesses the excellent state fully and automatically without conscious effort when they step into the pillar.
   b.) If A or B is not satisfied with the level of feeling accessed, go back to step 3-4 and add color, movement, sparkles, etc.

7. **Separator State**
"**Step back out of the pillar.**" (Ask neutral question)

8. **Desired Context**
"Now think of a future situation, or a context, where you would like to have more of this particular state of excellence."

9. **Separator State** (Break the "Desired Context" state with a neutral question.)

10. **Pair Context with Anchor**
"When I touch your shoulder, I want you to immediately step forward into the pillar and re-experience that excellent state. (pause) *Now think of that context or situation* (short pause) *where you want to have more of THIS* <touch shoulder, they step into pillar> *excellent state available."*

    B asks A:
    "How is it different with these resources available?"
    "How, specifically, could things go wrong in that future situation?"
    "What will let you know it's time to have these resources available?"

    (B observes to be sure that A quickly accesses the state of excellence.)

11. **Testing**
Ask A to step back out of the pillar. Then ask A to say a little about the future situation in order to get A to think about it and access it. *"Where will that future situation occur?"* or *"Who else will be there in that future situation?"* Observe to be sure that A only briefly accesses the problem state and then automatically accesses the state of excellence. You can also ask for verbal descriptions, but nonverbal communication is more important.

Practicing

You can practice anchoring relaxed states. You can also practice anchoring what it feels like to laugh at a good joke. You can anchor in yourself a state of mental alertness, and then fire an anchor for a state of physical relaxation. There are almost no limits on the ways in which you can apply anchoring. Experiment for yourself and see what states most help you get through your work, through your life, with enjoyment and efficiency.

Where Can I Use this Information?
- What state(s) would you like to be in when you are at work?
    - Access or create a state – Link to a unique finger 3x
    - Pair the state with the sight of your desk/tools/supplies/office

- What state(s) would you like to be in when you arrive home to your family/space?
    - Access or create a state – Link to another unique finger 3 times.
    - Pair state with the sight of the front door/entryway of your home.

- What state(s) would you like to be in when you are looking into the eyes of someone you love?

- How could you make use of the research that shows simply writing a list of things you are grateful for in life makes you likely to rate yourself as happier than if you have never written such a list?

    - Did you know that just remembering things for which you are grateful before you go to sleep at night is also scientifically proven to make you happier?

- How could you use your knowledge of anchoring to get better at falling asleep at night?

Anchoring-Based NLP Techniques

Some of the most incredibly powerful interventions and changes you can make are accomplished by utilizing what seem like very small, very slight, and yet very significant shifts you can easily lead a person through covertly during a conversation. This will become clearer as you learn how to apply anchoring in more strategic and specific ways. You can help people to gather and generate resources in powerful ways that can support them in making the changes they want in their life.

Practice Exercises

One of the most important states we want you to have at your disposal is being disassociated, or what is called being in Observer position. This is the focus of the next two exercises. (Note: we use the term "disassociated" to keep therapists from freaking out and claiming we are teaching people to "have dissociative disorder." We are actually doing something quite different, and you can explain it to them if you can anchor them out of their panic state.)

Whenever you can see an image of yourself in an image you remember, that is a disassociated image. If you relive/re-see the experience as if you are seeing it through your own eyes – that is an associated image.

You can also deliberately "disassociate" by trying some of the invitations in the following exercise. When you are disassociated or being an objective observer, you are mildly curious, and simply watching/listening to a situation. If you are "observing" and you feel emotional reactions or "pulls" in different directions, those feelings should be moved over or "floated" over to self – so self can make better distinctions. Observers just observe and take in information.

Anchoring Disassociation Exercise

(Trios A, B and C. Rotate positions after 5 minutes.)
1. **Elicit Disassociation**

      B says to A:

      "Imagine you step backward outside of yourself. Look back and see yourself standing in front of you." or –

      "What would you see if you were literally a fly on the wall watching this room from up by the ceiling?" or –

      "Imagine you are sitting in a movie theater seat, and imagine you float up into the projection booth. See yourself down there sitting in the theater seat."

      B anchors this disassociated state with a precise touch on A's shoulder. Remember the exact location and pressure you used to anchor them so you can recreate it.

2. **Calibrate to A's disassociated state**

    (Be sure you are anchoring A disassociating from the context he/she is currently in.)

3. **Separator State** (Distract to any neutral state.)

4. **Testing**

    B fires disassociation anchor.
    B and C watch for sensory-based evidence of disassociated state in A. (Called calibrating)

Common Indicators of Disassociation

There are common indicators that a person is disassociated, or in Observer position:

1. The person's head often moves back slightly so their head is not jutting forward beyond their shoulders.

2. Lessening or shallowing of the person's breathing.

3. Relaxation of the facial muscles – less facial expression; flat or mask-like face.

4. The eyes often glaze over – move less, focus on no specific point in space.

5. Voice tone changes, usually flattens and has less inflection.

Look and listen for these specific changes in B to verify that B is disassociated.

To assure your NLP work is effective be sure and know how to distinguish when someone is disassociated versus they are associated. Some techniques only work when the person is disassociated. Other techniques only work when the person is associated.

Chaining From a Stuck State to Disassociation Exercise

(Same trios – A, B and C. Rotate positions after 5 minutes.)

1.) B tests A's disassociation anchor that was created in the previous exercise. Be sure to have a reliable disassociation anchor.

2.) Separator state/break their state – ask a distracting question.

3.) **Elicit a mild stuck state**
B says to A: *"Think of a situation in which you get stuck."*

4.) **Chain stuck state to disassociation**
As soon as A begins to access the stuck state, B fires the anchor for disassociation. B and C observe to confirm that A does access the disassociated state.

5.) Repeat steps 2 – 4 two more times, so that A chains a stuck state to disassociation three times.

6.) Separator state.

7.) B tests by saying to A, *"Think of the stuck state."*
B and C observe to confirm that A's initial access of the stuck state automatically chains to the disassociated state. (If not, recycle back to the previous exercise.)

Anchoring Resources to New Contexts Exercises

Behavioral Context Transfer Exercise

(New trios – A, B and C. Rotate positions after 10 minutes)

1. B quickly **chains a (new/different) stuck state to a disassociated state**, and tests this in A.

2. **A is to select a past resource state or behavior**.
"Review your own past behaviors in other contexts until you see a behavior (Y) that you think would be appropriate for that context (X) where you were stuck."

3. Have B **experiment** with "trying out" the resource behavior in context:
"See and hear yourself doing this behavior (Y) in that context (X) where you were stuck" (A remains disassociated)

4. **Ecology Check**
   "Does any part of you object to this change? Is that what you want?" "Is that satisfactory?" (If not, recycle back to step #2, picking a different behavior.)

5. **Re-Associate**
   "Step into that movie and feel what it's like to be in that experience as you do those behaviors in that context."
   B and C observe to be sure that A is definitely in a more resourceful state. (If not, recycle back to steps #2 and #3.)

6. **Ecology Check**
   "Does any part of you object to this change now? Do you still want to have this behavior in this situation?" (If not, recycle back to steps #2 and #3 to revise the behavior or to select a different behavior.)

7. **Test**
   "I'd like you to think about being in that situation where you used to be stuck."
   B and C observe to be sure that the stuck state chains through disassociation to the resourceful behavior.
   (It may be very difficult for A to even access the stuck state at this point.)

8. **Future Pace**
   "When is the next time you're likely to encounter one of those situations? I want you to think of what it is that you see, hear, or feel just before one of those situations where you want to have this behavior in the future. Give yourself a 'dress rehearsal' now of actually having this experience."

Borrowing New Behaviors Exercise

(Same trios. Rotate positions after 10 minutes)

1. B quickly does chaining from stuck state to disassociation in A. (Use a new content for the stuck state.)

2. A selects someone to model:
   B says to A:
   a. *"Think of someone else who can handle that kind of situation really well."*
   b. *"See that person doing different behaviors in that troublesome context."*
   c. *"Choose one or more of those behaviors that you think would be particularly appropriate for you to learn to use in_____ (that context)."*
   d. *"See and hear yourself doing those effective behaviors in that context."*

3. **Ecology Check**
   "Does any part of you object to actually carrying out those new behaviors in that context?"

4. **Re-Associate**
    "Now step into that movie and feel what it's like to be in that experience as you do those behaviors in that context."

5. **Ecology check**

6. **Test**
    "I'd like you to think about being in that situation where you used to be stuck."
    B and C observe to be sure that the stuck state chains through to the resourceful behavior and state.

7. **Future Pace**
    "When is the next time you're likely to encounter one of those situations? I want you to think of what it is that you see, hear, or feel just before one of those situations where you want to have this behavior in the future. Give yourself a 'dress rehearsal' now of actually having this experience."

Anchoring to Add Past and Future Resources

Change Personal History Exercise

(Trios, A, B and C. Rotate positions after 15 minutes.)

1. **Identify Un-Resourceful State**
    "Think of (remember) a time when things didn't happen the way you wanted them to, and you'd like to feel differently about that memory." Or, *"Think of a memory that you still think of from time to time, and it leaves you feeling in a way you'd rather not feel."*
    (A may go on to step #2 before you ask him/her to.)

2. **B accesses and anchors (Anchor #1) un-resourceful state in A:**
    "When you think of that memory now, do you still feel bad?"
    Or, *"How do you think about this memory when it bothers you?"*
    As A accesses this state, B anchors it with a touch, and calibrates to this state. (This state can be either associated or disassociated; however the person recalls the memory.)

3. **Separator State**

4. **B tests anchor #1**

5. **Separator State**

6. **Identify Resource**
    "What resourceful state (courage, humor, alertness, calmness, etc.) would have made it possible for you to have had a much more satisfying and useful experience in that situation?"

7. **B accesses and anchors (Anchor #2) a resourceful state in A**
"Think of a time when you experienced a lot of that resource."
As A accesses the resource, make sure he/she is associated into it, with a full response, and anchor it with a different touch. Calibrate to this state.

8. **Separator State**

9. **B tests anchor #2**

10. **Separator State**

11. **Integration**
"Take this resource (B fires Anchor #2) back into that problem memory (B fires A's anchor #1) and find out what happens with this resource fully available to you. Watch and listen to all that happens as you relive that old experience in a new way. Take all the time you need, and let me know when you're done."
Calibrate to the integrated state that develops as the two states mix. (This time you want A to re-associate into the un-resourceful state as well as into the resourceful state.)

12. **Separator State**

13. **Test Integration**
B fires Anchor #1, or asks about the problem memory, and observe A's response.
(If you get the un-resourceful state response, rather than the integrated response, recycle back to re-anchor the resource, choose a more powerful, different or additional resource.)

14. **Future-Pace**
"Think about the next time you might encounter one of those situations in the future, (B fires A's anchor #2) *knowing fully that you have this resource available to you."*

Stretch: Do the pattern covertly.
Keep in mind that what is overt and obvious to you now as a result of this training will still be covert for most people!

One of my favorite applications of anchoring presented itself to me when I completed my five-week NLP Practitioner training and returned to working in the State psychiatric hospital. I returned from my "vacation" and was greeted by my very friendly co-workers. We were all sitting in the nursing station. They were smiling at me, and asking me about my training, and then a severely mentally ill patient approached the nursing station. In order to communicate with the staff, patients had to slide over a small sliding window and talk through it. The window made a "whooshing" sound and a "bang" each time it opened.

Having become sensitive to anchors in the world around me, I suddenly realized that the smiles on my fellow staff members diminished every time they heard this window open! So, I moved over to sit beside the window, and began to tell some great jokes I learned at the training. Each time they laughed, I would say, "Ka pow!!" as I slid the window open and produced the "Whoosh and bang" sound while they laughed. I wasn't sure it would work, so I told probably 15 jokes, firing this "sound effect anchor" each and every time. The impact was nothing short of amazing. Staff began to SMILE when that window slid open. This massively changed patient interactions in less than five minutes – because instead of that sound irritating staff, it entertained them – and they had a completely different start to all of their patient interactions.

I thought this would only last a short time. It lasted for years! I remember about a month after building this anchor, a staff member smiled when the window opened and said, "I don't know what the deal is, but we seem to have the most pleasant batch of patients we've had in years here lately!" I had to run from the nursing station so he wouldn't see me laughing.

This is why I always tell people you can get massive changes from very small and simple processes if you utilize them strategically.

Section 3: Beliefs

Why Do People Build Beliefs?

Why Intentionally Build Beliefs?

Some people are willing to live and die for their beliefs. Our beliefs guide what we will value - what will be important to us. Our beliefs also tell us what to want. But how do we know what to believe? And why do we even build beliefs in the first place?

There have been dozens of theories about how we build beliefs and belief structures. Most of them never answered a very simple question – why build belief structures at all? After all, if Freud was right and we are a sack of urges navigating a sea of culture, then why didn't our alleged primitive ancestors not just lay in the warm grass (comfort or shelter) next to their mates (urges), arm's length from a clear pool (water), in the shade of a fruit tree (food)? If psychology's teaching that all behavior is "need driven" is true, then we humans must have "higher needs" than just "the basics." (Maslow's Hierarchy of Needs?) Without some type of "higher needs" we would not evolve, and we would never withstand the insane, random rule structures known as our culture in attempts to meet our needs.

The most reasonable theory I have ever heard of the many I have studied comes from George A. Kelly, and was written up by him as a book entitled, "A Theory of Personality." [W. W. Norton and Company Inc. New York NY, 10110, 1955] Let me just be quick to say this incredible genius has STILL not been properly credited for what he did. His theory of personality states that the reason we build belief structures is because we want to increase the predictability of our world. I agree with this notion – in fact I believe this is one of our brain's most basic instincts.

This need to be able to predict events, understand circumstances and control what happens to us drove primitives to evolve. If we could not find the perfect setting listed above, we had to develop a way to make SURE water would get to us, and food would be available. We started to do actions like putting things in a sack and carrying them with us so we could predict we would have something to eat and drink later. Once we knew we had control of the "food and water" situation/domain for a while, we could sit up and walk around the strange world we lived in and investigate satisfying more and more abstract urges and wants. Soon, we were taking care of the food, water, air, and other needs in different environments, so we could send people to the moon and under the sea. It is our ability to anticipate what we will need that has allowed us to grow and evolve. We "set down a stake" in a fact or belief or way of thinking and behaving, and THEN we venture out to new ideas and territories. We always relate one idea to another in a **chain, sequence or metaphor.** This allows us to build maps in our head that allow us to navigate through the world.

However, as our beliefs become less concrete, our urges become more and more abstract. Nowadays we have gotten to the point where people literally kill themselves, or have children, or kill others because of simple mental structures called beliefs. This is why I felt compelled to write a book on belief structures. I spent many years working with severely mentally ill patients, assessing and treating "insanity." As an expert on insanity, I think society is going insane when we start to kill things because of ideas in ours minds that are in no way a threat or a problem to our actual physical well-being. The fact that it has been going on since the dawn of history is no excuse to continue.

Another very interesting notion in Kelly's theory is that "truth" or "factualness" is pretty much irrelevant. What IS relevant is if a belief increases the predictability of the world. This is why we believe things that we often know are "not true." For example, I may have had a terrible incident with a snake when I was a child. In that incident, I may have become so fearful that I lost control and ran home screaming in terror, and had to be "put back together" by my mother or another person. (i.e. "Son, you are back in the safe and predictable space of my home/presence/world…" Then I can get myself back to the belief, "World = safe place" again.) If it was a really bad incident, my brain may work VERY HARD to make absolutely certain that I never have another such incident with a snake. And just to be sure, I will develop a phobia of snakes. I may come to learn that snakes in fact are not "actually" very dangerous. However, in my world, in order to avoid a total fear breakdown, we must avoid snakes. I may "know" they are not dangerous, but still the belief drives my behavior.

By avoiding snakes, or other causes of uncertainty in our world, we carve out a "best truth." One of the things Kelly taught was that **we do not need to have a total understanding of the world, only enough of a map to be functional in our environment and satisfy our needs.**

One of my former jobs was assessing patients who came into the mental health facility with criminal charges to see if they were "faking" having a mental illness. While many people thought they would get "less time" for a crime if they were found insane, I knew this belief was not founded in reality. This assessment was actually rather simple. No matter how insane a person was, their insanity always had an "internal coherence," and they could link together all of those bizarre thoughts and beliefs into a system that held together. It didn't always withstand what is called "reality testing," but there was always an internal coherence. Even the most bizarre beliefs had to "make sense." No matter how much you misinterpret the world (and we all do), it must somehow be put together in a way that makes sense.

Thinking about Thinking

We humans have the incredible ability to think about our own thinking. Our brains not only notice patterns in the "outer" world, but we can notice patterns nested within patterns. These "meta-patterns" are why we are fascinated with fractals, with well-composed music, and with art. It is the ability to notice patterns that made us evolve so quickly.

There are as many ways to divide thinking and experience as there are experiences and thoughts. In keeping with Kelly's value of predictability, I have been searching for different maps of human behavior and treatment that actually could apply strategic interventions and produce predictable results. One of my favorites is Neuro-Linguistic Programming or NLP. One of the basic ideas in NLP is that there are only five senses through which we take in information. Thus, the basis of all of our higher-order thinking must still rest on lower-order, sensory-based elements. NLP was one of the first fields or disciplines to honor that people make images in their head and say things internally to themselves – and to treat these internal experiences as valid information! They were also unique in that the information ITSELF was considered as valid. They did not go an extra step and start attributing other causes or meanings to the images and the content of the voices. If you reported that you speak to yourself in a critical voice inside your head to a traditional therapist, most often they would try to make that voice come from one of your parents, or from a repressed personality, or from an alien from Planet Claire you are channeling. In my opinion the whole field of therapy becomes absolutely stupid at this "it means" level of the work. Millions of therapists have made careers out of "one upping" each other for the most abstract and bizarre (but inclusive!) explanation of a person's (patient's) behavior. It was NLP that helped me realize that even if you did find some "cause" of something internal, knowing the cause doesn't do a darn thing to help change it!

NLP also helped me learn that believing is one of the most random events in the universe. And, that people's beliefs could be changed very easily. If you don't believe me, quit now. Because that is what the rest of this book is about.

Beliefs Get "Paired" with States

Whenever we form or "borrow" a belief, we also attach an emotional component to that belief. This is one way we create prejudice. Often someone tells us a fact, and we have to question what emotional reaction they are trying to have accompany that belief. How many times has someone said something to you like, "John has three children!" with a rather emphatic voice tone, and you looked at them questioningly and said or thought to yourself, "That's GOOD, right?" They may explain that children are very important to them, and that they think it is wonderful that such a nice man has three children. Or, they may go on about how John really doesn't make enough money to "properly" support that many children. Either way, you may seek clarification from them about what emotional "tag" they put onto that belief. Almost every belief we have includes an emotional tag. Beliefs that lack emotional tags are actually very rare. And our emotional tags can come from a variety of sources.

If I talk with someone on the phone and I become upset and angry, and ten seconds later you come into my office and tell me about John having three kids, my state of being upset and angry may "flavor" my interpretation of what you are telling me about John. Even though you MAY be trying to tell me, "It is good that such a nice man has three children," my emotional state may lean me toward forming the belief, "He doesn't make enough money to support that many kids." This is another way that our emotional states can actually change or "flavor" beliefs.

Wars are fought over beliefs. Fears arise from beliefs. Love and romance grow out of beliefs. The entire emotional gamut gets run as we go through a person's belief system. Philosophy and logic are geared toward "pure reasoning." However, we human beings very rarely get involved in "pure" reasoning." Instead, we package our beliefs and emotional states together, and most often deliver them to others in these "packages." We can influence others to pair a belief with a positive emotion, and this produces positive prejudice. Or, we can influence others to pair a belief with negative connotations, and this is how we get negative prejudice. Keep in mind that nearly all beliefs carry an emotional component.

The Three Sources of Beliefs

It is this writer's belief that **believing is one of the most random events in the universe.** In other words, who decides our facts and who decides our fictions is a completely arbitrary process, though we all rely on a "feeling of certainty."

I like to think of beliefs being formed or "sculpted" over time. Sometimes they form slowly, and sometimes they form quickly. There seem to be three main ways that beliefs are formed.

1.) One of the ways people learn to believe information is when it is repeatedly "tapped" into them on a frequent basis – in other words, by their **culture or environment**. Being raised in any kind of family delivers to us a set of values and "ideals." We often spend our lives trying to fulfill (or trying to rebel against) our parents' values. Either way, the beliefs and values in which we are immersed are often adopted unconsciously. By living in a commune or belonging to a church, being around others who share our beliefs helps to reinforce and to shape them. This is like sculpting by using little, persistent chips.

One interesting aspect of this cultural influence is that "cultural carriers" such as newspapers, magazines and television inherently value certain messages and simply do not carry other messages. Nobody on the evening news will ever tell you, "Everything is alright. You are safe. All is right in the world. Have a good night." But certainly they would love to inform you of the latest threats to your well-being that they have uncovered! Our culture tells us a great deal about what to consider important, and what to ignore. Unfortunately, the values that our culture thereby labels as important are not always useful for us as individuals or as a society.

2.) A second way people often accept or believe information (that happens more quickly) is when it **comes from an expert.** When you are a parent, you generally have the powerful combined influence of these first two always present – until your children become adolescents. At that point, they generally choose some deranged, drug-abusing musician to be their preferred expert from whom they will accept values and information.

This is like sculpting using a mold. The entire belief is adopted, "as is" – no building process. Beliefs adopted in this manner are often "tweaked" and adapted slightly later, so that they survive in our individual belief structures. Or, they can result in huge shifts in an individual's entire belief structure. That means the person chose to adjust all of their **other** related beliefs, so they could adopt the expert's belief completely! (That generally indicates a great deal of trust in them as an authority, or some other outcome such as being liked by them, or even being, " just like them…")

3.) Beliefs are often adopted very quickly during extremely **intense experiences.** People have what they call, "Defining Moments." Most people over the age of 10 can tell you of some "defining moment" they have experienced – where they made some kind of decision, and they changed from that point onward. Perhaps something happened that changed how they define the world, or how they define themselves. Going to dinner to celebrate the beginning or ending of something, or announcing a change over a toast are both rituals designed to create defining moments. If the stage is further set with intense emotion, ideas can get emotionally super-charged and therefore become "extremely believed." Beliefs formed in this way are often powerful influences. Neuro-Linguistic Programming (NLP) utilizes a fabulous method called reimprinting for helping uncover and change beliefs formed in this way. In the hands of a highly skilled NLP Practitioner, reimprinting can quickly change your life!

An amazing variety of beliefs get created in this way. For example, a friend of mine stated that when he was 10 years old, his 12-year-old brother died. While he was very sad about losing his brother, when the family told him the news, the fact that most stood out in his mind at that moment was, "Oh my God! This 'dying and going away forever' thing is going to happen to ME too!" He said that ever since that moment, he has been aware that his death is always "just around the corner." Notice the phrase he used? His older brother was killed when he was hit by a car as it turned around a corner.

If we continue to use the metaphor of sculpting for "extreme experience" beliefs, I would say this would be sculpting by using explosives! You get a lot of really powerful and intense shapes (really significant and influential beliefs), but you never know what you are going to end up with until after the explosion happens, and sometimes a lot of other stuff (another belief) gets injured or killed in the explosion/formation process.

In addition to forming from intense emotions, beliefs are also strongly influenced by our general **emotional states and experiences**. While we don't like to admit it, our beliefs can easily be altered by our mood, by changes in the environment, and by a variety of other factors.

As we begin to alter and play with beliefs, you will begin to gain control of the direction of your life, without the need for extreme discipline, intense motivation, or even much effort. When all of your beliefs and values are in alignment, things like discipline, motivation and where to focus your efforts just naturally happen. Sometimes you have to "nudge up your motivation," but for the most part, you can function incredibly well on autopilot when you have your goals and values in alignment with your daily beliefs.

Now that we know about the most common sources of beliefs (that is, if you believe the above material, and even if you don't), let's explore more about beliefs. We will begin using a model to diagram the structure of people's values and beliefs that I learned from Charles Faulkner in his Perceptual Cybernetics™ training in 1994. Let's start with a simple example, and use the model to show how the belief building process works.

The Structure of Beliefs

What is a Frame?

When you place a painting or a picture in a frame, the frame is expected to enhance the picture by being a sort of background. We have all seen badly framed pictures - where either there was too much frame, or not enough frame, or the frame and picture simply did not go together. The frame helps create a setting for a picture to "happen" within.

People have their beliefs in frames or domains. These domains have sub-groupings that are different for each person. Part of how we build rapport with a person at a deeper level is by matching their domain sub-structures.

For example, I know a bit about music. I consider my music domain to be very large. But if you ask me about the latest popular group on the radio and the name of their hit song, I will not know it. I do not consider "Latest Pop Group's Song" as an important sub-grouping. However, if you ask me to sing you a German augmented 6th chord, I will ask you for the tonic note from which to start singing. I have a degree in music theory, and I am a musician. I have to know how to calculate that chord in any key. So I have a sub-grouping called, "Calculations for the German Augmented 6th chord." For other people, "Cassettes, Radio Stations and old 45-songs" represents their entire music domain. We may think we are having a conversation about "music," but what I think of when you mention that word is different than what you think of when you mention that word. Nevertheless, we may be having a conversation that we would both label being about music. If we decide we are having a conversation about music, then music could be the "frame" of our conversation. **In terms of beliefs, a frame is the context.**

We would not look at each other during our music conversation and say, "Hey, we are having a conversation about music." That would be "naming the frame." If one of us did that, we would probably proceed to a conversation about what each of us considers to be music, or about our other hobbies. If you "name the frame," the frame automatically shifts. When you name the frame, it becomes content. Once the frame becomes content, our consciousness shifts to the next larger frame, or to another/lateral frame.

Sometimes you want to name the frame, other times you don't. Doesn't that help?

But think about this... The element in any multi-leveled system with the most frame-shifting flexibility has a distinct advantage. If you know your NLP presuppositions, you know what that advantage is called - control.

First let's go to an example about frames.

An Example of Frames:

In the world of retail sales, when you start the buying process with a customer, you must first qualify them and find out their purchasing criteria. A good salesperson asks questions to uncover your needs, and uses their knowledge of products to persuade you to buy the one that will fulfill those needs.

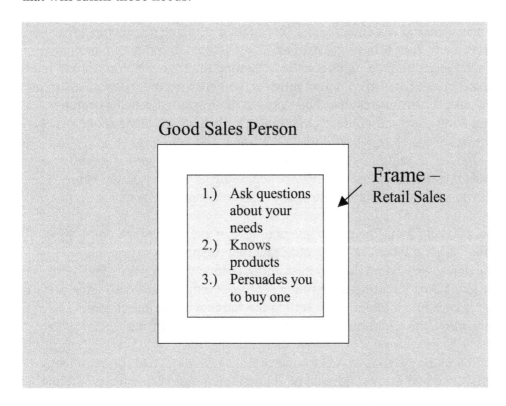

Good Sales Person

1.) Ask questions about your needs
2.) Knows products
3.) Persuades you to buy one

Frame –
Retail Sales

Now stop and examine what I have just written above this diagram, and notice the relationships diagrammed above, as I "talk about what I just talked about..."

In the above discussion of a sales person, the "frame" is retail sales. Often in written text, the frame is "set" by the first line of a paragraph, or by changing the size of text - as was done here with "An Example of Frames:" - to set off this retail sales example. In conversation, people often have a different voice tone or gesture when they are "marking a frame." You can learn to duplicate their set of behaviors associated with this shift to assist you in shifting frames with them. You can also use it as a cue or "anchor" when YOU want to shift frames.

In the above discussion of a sales person, the topic or entity we were discussing was "a good sales person." I used a set of "criteria" to describe or delineate expectations for a good sales person. Another way to phrase this is, "If these 3 criteria are met, you can call this sales person 'a good sales person.'" Yet another way to say this is, "In order to categorize this world event as an 'instance of good sales person,' the following 3 elements must be present."

(Right now I am not diagramming whether you believe this about sales people or not, I am just diagramming a single belief. You will just have to trust me about the criteria for a good sales person. I've worked in sales. I'm an expert. So you can trust me to help you form the belief…)

Let's go on to another example, and expand our diagram a little further.

Another Example of Frames

Let's say you are a manager, and it is time to do a six-month evaluation on an employee. You bring the employee into your office, and explain that you are doing their six-month evaluation for their work performance. This is called, "Setting the frame." You want to tell your employee an exact statement of the context in which you are meeting, because assuming the wrong frame can have disastrous results. This "stating the frame" also helps people to focus in on the information you want. Often we assume people have the same frame that we do. While it might be true, it is always useful to set the frame, to avoid any misunderstandings. In NLP training it is said, "An ounce of framing is worth a ton of reframing." You must mention the frame at the very beginning of the interaction in any interaction in which you want to maintain control or keep a very specific outcome.

By setting the frame, you help focus the entire interaction. For example, some employees assume they are being yelled at whenever they walk into their manager's office, and immediately become defensive. Some therapy customers assume that they are "faulty" or "defective" and that like a doctor cutting out a tumor, you are going to "cut out" some part of their personality that is causing a problem. By setting the frame with an initial context statement, you help to eliminate a number of possible communication difficulties.

For managers, we will assume a frame of "Performance Improvement," and for treatment professionals/therapists, we will assume a frame of "Functioning more effectively." While these words sound very similar to each other, a simple example will show us how quickly differences in the perceived frame influences our experience and behavior.

Mr. Smith and the Cellular Store

Imagine you are a manager of a cellular phone store, and you are about to do the six-month performance evaluation on a new employee, Mr. Smith. You review his record, and you also remember that you helped with his training, and he seemed to catch-on to the products well. However, Mr. Smith is chronically late, and in fact, is 30-minutes late getting to work 80% of the time (four days a week!). His co-workers are complaining about this, but otherwise he is an absolutely exemplary employee.

When Mr. Smith enters your office, you start by saying, "Good morning, Mr. Smith. I want to meet with you to do your six-month performance evaluation this morning. Are you ready to do that with me now?" This allows Mr. Smith to know what to expect from the meeting. It also tells him that now is not the time to complain about fellow employees, to go to lunch, or to wait on another customer in the store. By asking if he is ready to do that now, you are allowing him the opportunity to "make a choice." If he is in a bad mood, stressed from home situations, or otherwise distracted he may ask to do this with you another time. If he says he is ready, then you begin your evaluation.

In keeping with the frame of "Improving Performance," you FIRST review Mr. Smith's exemplary behaviors with him. As a manager, you have a certain set of expectations of employees. Another way of saying this would be to say that you have certain beliefs about how employees should behave. They may be your personal beliefs, or they may be spelled out in company policy. Let's say you have the following requirements:

1.) Good product knowledge
2.) Courteous to customers
3.) Does tasks as assigned
4.) Shows up for work on time

for someone to be considered a "good employee."

We can diagram this as:

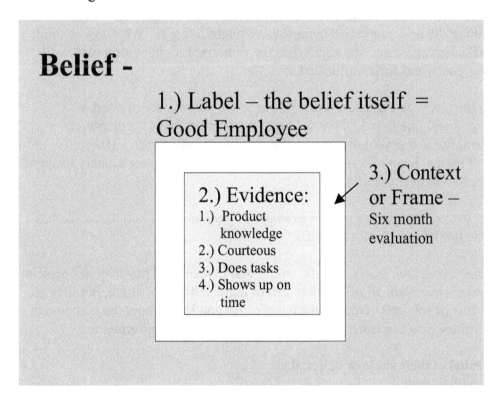

Belief -

1.) Label – the belief itself = Good Employee

2.) Evidence:
1.) Product knowledge
2.) Courteous
3.) Does tasks
4.) Shows up on time

3.) Context or Frame – Six month evaluation

What is diagrammed here is the thinking, "In the context of this six month evaluation, I must see the following four behaviors in order to rate you as a good employee." Given what we know of Mr. Smith, he has not met all of the criteria for a rating as a good employee at this time. No matter how polite, no matter how knowledgeable, no matter how on task he is, he has not met the criteria for "good employee rating" for this review period.

Here is where the "ethical dilemma" begins. Nowhere in the company policy, in the relationship between manager and supervisee, or in our culture does anything allow for, "But golly! I like Mr. Smith. I WANT him to get 'Good Employee.'" An ethical dilemma always involves things that are conflicting because of different "levels." We will begin to diagram levels of beliefs after we practice a little more with diagramming beliefs.

Let's diagram another example in the context of counseling.

Mrs. Jones and Her Failed Life

You are a therapist who has a new client come to your office.

Mrs. Jones told you on the phone that she is "depressed and wants counseling." In your initial interview, you ask her, "What's wrong?" She states that her husband ignores her and the family, she is frustrated in her current job, and she thinks her husband is having an affair. She describes her life as a "failure," and she claims this is the cause of her depression.

In the above scenario, Mrs. Jones believes her life is an example of a "Failed Life." People must have a belief that they are in a certain "state," or that they are an "instance" or "example" of something. So as a concerned therapist, we might ask her, "Why do you think your life is a failure?" Through tears, she states that she is married to the wrong man, will never meet her career goals, and feels unfulfilled.

As an objective therapist, we see that she is only 30-years old, very nicely dressed, and appears quite intelligent and functional. Thus we know that her thinking is completely psychotic, and we send her to a psychiatrist down the street for medication… (Having worked in the field of mental health for over 35 years, I know that this unfortunately happens more often than anyone will ever admit!)

Or, if you prefer, we can use her thinking as an example of diagramming beliefs, as she has given you an absolute gold mine of information.

People are always discussing their goals, beliefs, values and evidence. They may not present them in a specific order, or explain all of the elements of a given belief or value, but they are always referring to their beliefs and evidence for beliefs. As you learn about the component parts of beliefs and values, you can learn to distinguish if a person is mentioning the

> 1.) **label** of their value or belief, their
> 2.) **evidence** for it, or the
> 3.) **context** of it.

Fortunately, if you have taken certain NLP trainings, you already know the correct questions to ask to get each piece of information. They are parts of The Outcome Template you may have learned in NLP Practitioner (Basic) training:

- The question, **"What's important about that for you?"** asks for the belief or value, and what it is labeled. You could also ask, "What does that mean to you?"
  - It is an invitation to become more abstract.

- The question, **"How will you know when you have it?"** asks for the evidence.
    - It is an invitation to become more specific.

- The question, **"Where, when and with whom do you want this?"** asks for the context or frame.

Let's start with her "complaint."

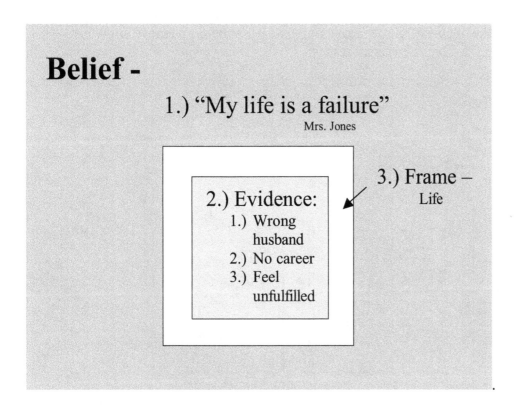

Belief -

1.) "My life is a failure"
Mrs. Jones

2.) Evidence:
1.) Wrong husband
2.) No career
3.) Feel unfulfilled

3.) Frame –
Life

The first distinction we need to make is that all of these statements are being made in the negative. We have no listed "targets," goals, or objectives. We have instead, a list of what is NOT present. If our customer is unmotivated, depressed, or untrusting this is often very likely. We can simply notice this, and then ask questions to clarify. We need to also note that the question we asked was, "What's wrong?" This is certainly an appropriate response to that **extremely non-useful question**.

There is a MAJOR shift happening in the therapeutic world where instead of being focused on the PROBLEMS, we shift our focus to the SOLUTIONS! You cannot imagine how violently opposed most therapists are to this shift. Most therapists have made their careers out of "wallowing in people's problems," and if you try to shift the focus to solutions, they accuse you of being "in denial" and of trying to gloss over the client's problems. It is a totally different approach to problems that is barely gaining any recognition or acceptance.

In a non-problem focus, we first ask the customer or client to develop a goal that is stated in the positive, and determine if they want that as an outcome. The same is true in identifying and working with beliefs - we need to uncover what IS evidence for different things – what IS an instance of something - not what is missing in the situation. Steve Andreas once said, "If you get in a taxi and you say, 'I don't want to go to Miami, I don't want to go to Cleveland, I don't want to go to Texas… it will take a VERY long time to get to your destination. Instead, ask the person for a specific target.

We could ask Mrs. Jones, "So what you want is for your life to be a success, is that right?" **If** she agrees with our distorting backtrack, then we would ask for her evidence as to how she would know her life is a success. This evidence must also be stated in the positive. Let's say Mrs. Jones tells us the opposites, just to make our example simple. Then we know her evidence for thinking that her life is a success is:

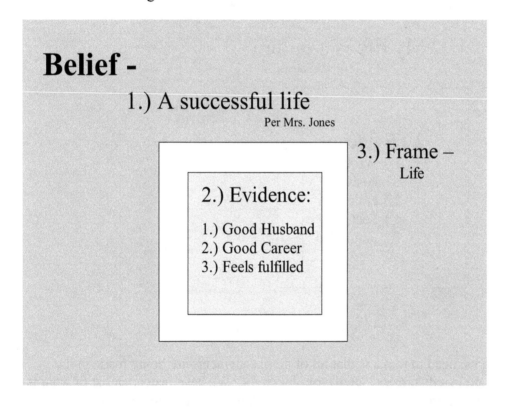

Levels of Abstraction

Mrs. Jones is exhibiting symptoms of a terrible disease called, "Abstractitis." When people have this disease, their mind becomes infected with abstract ideas that swell-up and take up more and more of their thinking. It is often a side effect of too much education, too much therapy, or simply a communication style. The only way to treat this disease is with a lot of rapport, a lot of patience, and some very strategic questions.

Each time you have asked for evidence, Mrs. Jones has offered another "abstraction." There is still no mention of any behavior you can see, any words that can be heard, or any specific directions for change.

The main difference between management and counseling is in the level of abstraction or the "size of the frame" you work with. In management, you want to help someone function more effectively in the context of the company for which you both work. That context or frame does not change throughout your relationship with your employee. However, in counseling, people often want you to help make their "life" better. This frame is very large, and we must ask questions to find out the evidence that supports such beliefs. Often the evidence is also abstract, and again, we must ask for another level of evidence. If Mrs. Jones states that she wants a good husband as part of a successful life, we can ask her, "How would you know when you have a good husband?" Let's imagine she replies, "A good husband would share the time with the kids, and would want to be with his wife." We could diagram her response as follows:

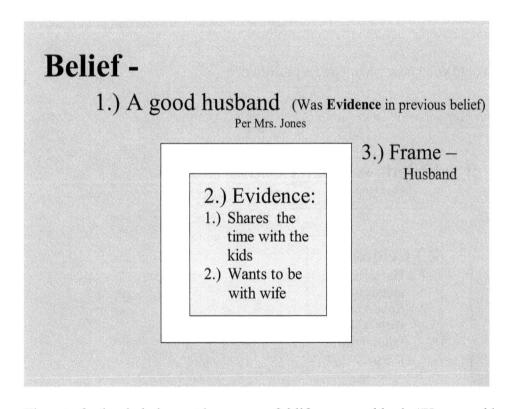

Belief -

1.) A good husband (Was **Evidence** in previous belief)
Per Mrs. Jones

3.) Frame –
Husband

2.) Evidence:
1.) Shares the time with the kids
2.) Wants to be with wife

Then, to further help her get her successful life, we would ask, "How would you know when you had a good career?" Let's imagine she responds, "I would earn at least $75,000.00 per year salary." Again, we would diagram this as:

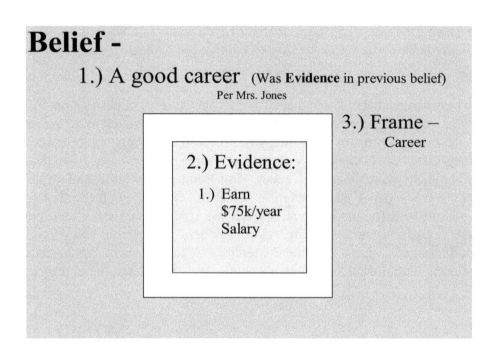

And finally "How would you know when you feel fulfilled?"

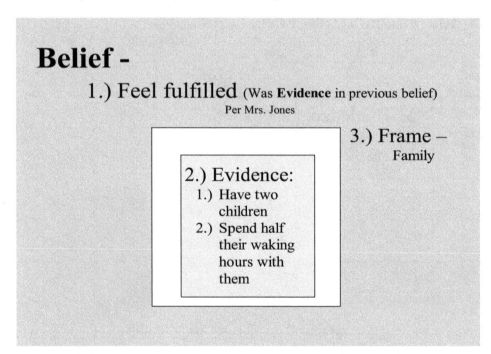

Notice that the abstraction "Feel fulfilled" had as criteria what many people would call, "Raising a family." This type of shift to more specific evidence often happens when we ask people to begin to state things in the positive.

And finally, we could diagram what we know about her belief system so far:

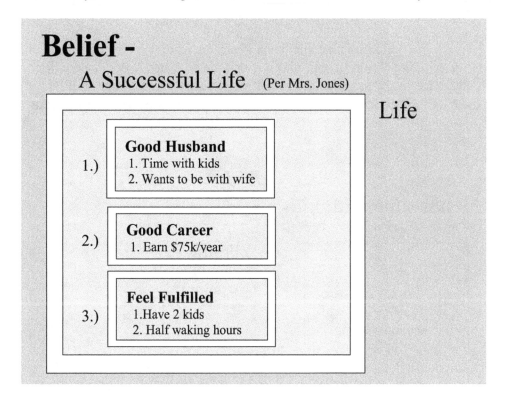

These are called, "Nested beliefs" or "nested evidence." The higher the level of abstraction (the more abstract), the more layers of nesting will take place. How do you know when you are appropriately digging down into layers of abstraction?

The Evidence for Evidence

You keep asking for evidence until you get:

V= Visual Evidence

Something you/they can see with your eyes

A= Auditory Evidence

Something you/they can hear with your ears

K= Kinesthetic Evidence

Something you/they can feel in your body

Evidence can also be something you smell or taste. However, this is much less likely. If the evidence is not sensory specific, then it is an abstraction. If it is an abstraction, then we need to keep asking for the evidence for the abstraction. Since Mrs. Jones' evidence is not completely sensory specific yet, we still need to ask more questions. So, let's start with first asking more about her two requirements for a good husband.

She has already told us that she will know that she has a good husband, "…When I find a man who will spend time with the children, and who wants to be with me." We can ask for her to further specify the evidence by saying, "What will you see, hear or feel that will let you know that your husband is spending time with the kids?" she may provide the following criteria:

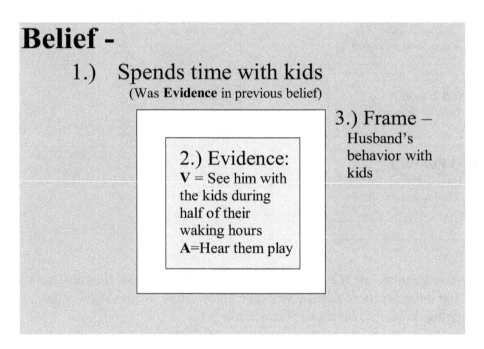

Belief -
1.) Spends time with kids
(Was **Evidence** in previous belief)

2.) Evidence:
V = See him with the kids during half of their waking hours
A=Hear them play

3.) Frame –
Husband's behavior with kids

She needs to both **see** him with the kids for a certain number of hours a day, and to **hear** them play together. In the context of employment, these are called, "Performance Objectives." The process is no different in human life than in the frame of employment. Certain events must happen in the world for people to be convinced that an example of something just occurred. And how we structure the requirements of "an example of X" appears to be unique for every individual. This disagreement about "sufficient evidence" can produce some strange consequences. For Mrs. Jones – what if her husband takes the children down the street to a park to play? Then she neither sees nor hears them playing! So would her husband still be meeting her criteria of spending time with the children? Actually -NO! Her evidence is seeing and hearing them play. If he came home and stated that he had spent 10 hours with the children, it STILL would not meet her criteria. She might SAY that is good and might even try to think or believe that he spent time with the children, but she will not feel fully convinced that he really did. Because, after all, she did not hear or see them playing together!

Let's use an example.

In order for Mrs. Jones to believe that she has a good husband, the other criteria/required evidence was that he "want to be with her." Once again, there is no sensory specific example or evidence, so we ask, "How do you know when your husband wants to be with you?" At this point, people often talk a lot, but what you are waiting for is the simple, sensory specific experiences. You can always ask, "What will you see, hear or feel that will let you know…" Most often, people are waiting for a certain look from their spouse, or a remark, or a particular voice tone, or a particular hug. Mrs. Jones finally decided that she felt "wanted" when her husband gave her a specific look, and when they spent time together alone at least once a week. We diagram this as:

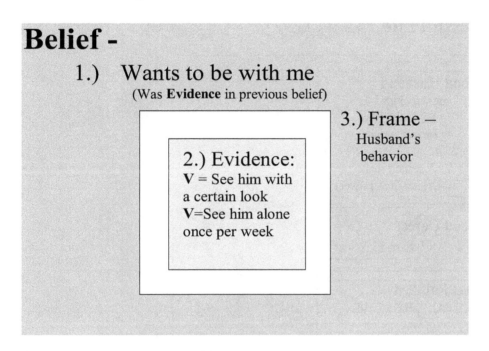

Belief –

1.) Wants to be with me
(Was **Evidence** in previous belief)

2.) Evidence:
V = See him with a certain look
V=See him alone once per week

3.) Frame –
Husband's behavior

While people don't like to think that "feeling wanted" (or even "feeling loved") is as simple as "getting a particular look from a particular person," it actually is! Most people don't object to that idea about other people's beliefs, but they don't like it about their own beliefs. And by the way – if you happen to use this information in your life and your spouse has told you how they know you love them, be sure and provide them with that evidence just the way they want it, and quite frequently. In fact, practice getting better at it! For example, if your spouse says they know you love them by a certain look you give them, ask them to "point out" that look when you do it to them. Then, work with them to see if you can make tiny adjustments to that look to make them feel even MORE loved. Imagine how nice it could be if you and your spouse PRACTICED making the other feel deeply loved!!

Now let's return to Mrs. Jones…
Her second criterion for a successful life was that she had a good career, and she stated that her evidence was making $75,000.00 per year. All we need to make it sensory specific is to ask, "Would you see that number in the bank, or on a tax form, or your paycheck? What would let you know you made $75,000.00 in a year?" As long as she provides reasonable and sensory-based criteria and not, "My uncle says I make that much," we can move on.

Her third criterion was that she could raise a family. She reports that she already has two children. Again, if we ask her how she knows this, it may be absurd. But notice she also has listed as her criteria that she herself spends half of the children's waking hours with them.

In order to diagram the entire belief structure that was given to us in the first thirty seconds of interaction with Mrs. Jones, three levels of abstraction/investigation are required to reach sensory specific data. This "belief nest" is diagrammed as shown:

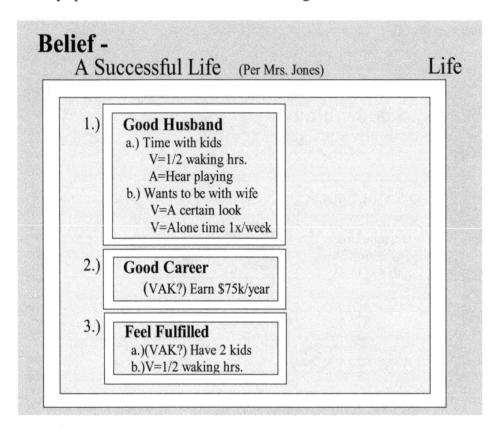

Belief -
A Successful Life (Per Mrs. Jones)   Life

1.) **Good Husband**
   a.) Time with kids
       V=1/2 waking hrs.
       A=Hear playing
   b.) Wants to be with wife
       V=A certain look
       V=Alone time 1x/week

2.) **Good Career**
   (VAK?) Earn $75k/year

3.) **Feel Fulfilled**
   a.)(VAK?) Have 2 kids
   b.)V=1/2 waking hrs.

We have used belief diagrams to show how "simple beliefs" have only one level – some evidence equals some event. We moved on to diagramming more complex beliefs, where beliefs and their evidence are "nested" within different beliefs. In these nests, all of the evidence must be present in order to claim that the event exists in the world. Sometimes, we want - but don't REQUIRE - that every bit of evidence be present. Sometimes, a particular piece of evidence may have more "weight" or importance than another. These are called values. We can apply this same type of diagram to values, and learn to appreciate how different belief structures can interact and influence each other.

Values

Sometimes a customer offers their beliefs, but they are stated as values. This same system is used to diagram values. Values are simply beliefs that have been ranked in importance. In the prior example, we had a list of evidence or criteria for "a successful life." However, Mrs. Jones did not say that any one of those pieces of evidence was more important than the others. We thus labeled her belief system as "nested." There was no more or less important belief. All seemed equally important. If your system of beliefs is prioritized, you describe your beliefs as values.

Let's diagram an example of values.

In this example, you are hiring a secretary for your office. You have decided that you want someone who will treat customers with respect, because that is the most important value to you. So during the interviews with potential candidates, you will be alert for evidence of respect. It's pretty obvious what respect is, isn't it?

No, it most certainly is not! When we get to vague values like "respect," evidence can vary tremendously from person to person. All evidence is sensory-based – something we see, hear, or feel. In the case of respect, we may look for such evidence as:

    1.) Good eye contact
    2.) Well groomed
    3.) Sits still while being spoken to

We may also want to hear specific evidence, such as:

    1.) Clear speaking voice
    2.) Good vocabulary

And we may even want to feel some specific feeling, for example:

    2.) I feel comfortable in his/her presence

We could diagram our value of respect in this way:

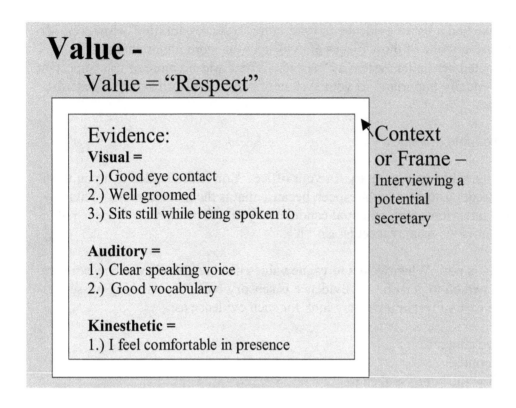

One beautiful aspect of "cultural diversity training" is that it is helping us realize that different people utilize different evidence for the same "qualities" or values. For example, holding eye contact is considered extremely disrespectful in some cultures, where the individual with less status generally looks to the floor to indicate deference to the authority. In some cultures, a very low speaking voice is a way of showing respect for authority. And to still other cultures, sitting very still while being spoken to can indicate a lack of interest.

Is evidence really so important? Try the simple example. We had suggested doing it previously, and will be more explicit about now. (Do you get the point that we want you to do this!!) Go home, and ask your spouse or friend, "How do you know that I love you?" You can also ask, "What lets you know that I love you?" Your spouse will respond with either visual, auditory or kinesthetic evidence. Some spouses reply, "I know by how you look at me." (Visual evidence) Some spouses may reply, "Because you tell me so." (Auditory evidence) Some spouses may say, "By how I feel when you are around." (Kinesthetic evidence) As we mentioned, we all would like to think that "abstract" values like "love" and "honesty" are not so "easy," but remember that we all have simple evidence procedures that help us to decide that certain qualities and values are present in the world around us.

While you are "qualifying customers" by finding out what they want and what they value, it is important that you accurately gather the EVIDENCE they will use, not just the values and beliefs and their labels which is what therapists so often do. You will use the label section later, but for now, focus on the evidence section.

IMPORTANT RULE: Always, always show respect for people's evidence or values.

If your spouse indicates to you the specific look that means to them, "I love you," you simply want to support them in feeling loved. You would never want to say something like, "That's it? All I have to do is this silly look and you feel loved??" At the level of "evidence," you can make adjustments, ask questions, and ask for coaching. You can even suggest to people that they change their evidence. But if you just question the evidence and the belief or value that the person has "put together" in their experience, you are in for major rapport problems.

People do not like their evidence to be challenged, and they do not like to have to "defend" their beliefs. Approach the whole thing with sensitivity and curiosity. People will be glad to share their evidence and their beliefs with you – as long as you don't communicate that you disagree!! Even if you DO disagree, you must do so gently and with rapport so the other person does not "recoil" at your questions about their beliefs.

Beliefs and Values

Whenever we have a system of values, we have a series of beliefs and evidence that are prioritized. We literally give more "weight" or credibility to some pieces of evidence than others. We are willing to count the presence of one of these more important pieces of evidence as sufficient evidence to believe the quality exists.

For example, let's say that Mrs. Jones applies for our secretarial position, as it pays $75,000.00 per year. She interviews, and meets all your criteria for respect. She is hired under your recommendation. Later the rest of the office staff meets her. They find her depressing and difficult to be around, but she is a good worker. It is quite likely that Mrs. Jones met the criteria for grooming, eye contact and sitting still, as well as having an excellent vocabulary and clear speaking voice. And while she did not meet the criteria of "comfortable to be around," you adjusted the "value," the "weight", or the "influence level" of "comfortable to be around" in your final decision.

We can notice the same process with an earlier example you may remember. Mr. Smith was an exemplary employee in our cellular store, but we could not give him the "Good Employee" rating, because he was late for work so frequently. We would have to adjust the "value level" of his tardiness. We might feel like we should "cut him some slack," and simply tell him his tardiness is a problem that must be changed by his next review. This kind of change in evidence/values is easier in a social relationship than it is in an employee relationship. The "standards" should not be easily bent in the work environment. The "bendability of standards" is a personal choice in social relationships, and a major indicator of compatibility in relationships too!

Values and Meaning

We have been examining information from a variety of different "levels." We have considered evidence as being something visual, auditory or kinesthetic. We have reviewed setting "contexts" in which conversations take place – but did not discuss the actual people involved in the conversations. Because we humans are complex beings in a complex world, our internal maps are a wonderfully complex array of different levels of meaning. Whenever we label an experience, we give it a "meaning tag" or a name, we move "up" one level in abstraction. There can be many levels of abstraction, and again, matching the level of abstraction of a conversation is a major rapport builder.

Let's start with an example again.

Mrs. Jones actually needs only six different events to be present in the world in order for her to feel that her life is a success. She must:

See:	Hear:	Feel:
Herself with children ½ waking hours	Husband playing with children	Time alone with husband each week
Husband with children ½ waking hours		Earning $75K
Certain look received from husband during week		

It's scary, but life can actually be that simple – from a certain perspective…

In fact, the only real reasons, if you want to get down to empirical "evidence," that Mrs. Jones came to counseling was because she wasn't making enough money in her job, and her husband was not spending half of his waking hours with the children. She got her high-paying job, but now she still is not happy. But she could not just "complain" that her husband was not spending half of his waking hours with the children. In fact, she wasn't even aware that this was a problem - because the client doesn't experience it that way! They experience this simply as "failed life. The non-meeting of the lower criteria listed in her requirements for a successful life (diagram repeated here) caused her to "decide" that her life was a failure:

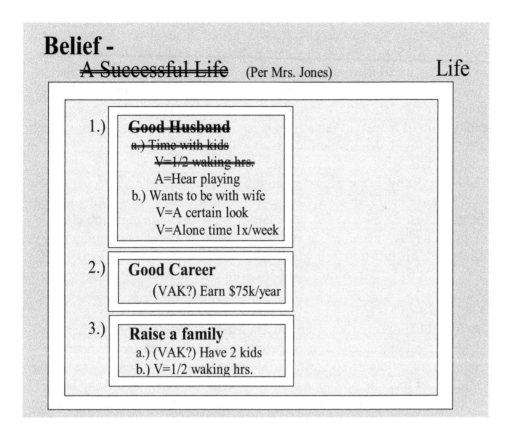

Now we know her evidence for her different beliefs, and we know that the world is not meeting one of her required pieces of evidence. We cannot shift evidence in this situation, so we must shift upward to attempting to shift her belief from a "higher level." Rather than changing or uncovering evidence, we are going to shift her labels or "meaning tags." This will involve some form of reframing, where we will change the meaning of the event, not the event or evidence itself.

We can move "upward" in abstraction by asking, "What's important about that for you?" If we ask this of Mrs. Jones, she replies, "I want my children to be in the safety of their parents care when they are awake. If I spend half my time with the children, and my husband spends half of his time with the children, then the children will always have supervision, and my husband will be sharing the parenting load fairly with me."

Mrs. Jones has introduced two "higher level" values from which she has "borrowed" criteria to form "Good Husband" ideals and "Safe Children" ideals. She has introduced another value of "husband shares parenting load fairly," and the evidence she has chosen is spends half of his time with the children. Again, this same behavior is being used as evidence in yet another belief, and this belief is even "higher order," or more important. If only her husband would spend those extra hours with those children!! If you remember, in her initial interview, she stated that her husband "ignores her and the family", she is "frustrated" in her current job, and she thinks her husband is having an affair. We took care of her job, but oh that husband!

Well, her husband is also having a "higher level values" conflict. It seems that he was raised in a culture where men were ABSOLUTELY expected to be able to provide for their family. His father taught him that, "… a real man provides for his family - a roof over their heads, food in their stomachs and… (fill in your own parent's expectations here)" And to NOT be able to provide for your family in HIS family meant you were a disgusting, useless pig, a non-human and a skanky glob of feces! In fact, there was nothing more shameful for a "real man" than not being able to provide for his family.

Well, with inflation and everything, her husband is having trouble making ends meet, and is embarrassed to tell her, because he doesn't want her to know how hard he is working to keep up with his half of the expenses. In fact, he has gone out to get a little part-time job at the local grocery store. Unfortunately, the schedule at the grocery store (which is helping him be a REAL MAN) conflicts with his full-time job working at the cellular store, and he is late for work 80% of the time! That's right; Mr. Smith and Mrs. Jones are married. Mrs. Jones kept her maiden name.

The point of this story is that beliefs are rather simple to diagram as we've seen. When we maneuver into values, things get extremely slippery, very quickly. Values are the result of ranking and prioritizing beliefs, evidence and criteria into networks and systems. We might be able to convince Mrs. Jones that she must change her criteria for "half the waking hours" to "90% of his non-working hours." Or, we could go to a "higher level belief" and work to convince her that her children ARE in fact, safe. And that since her husband is working 60 hours a week, he is "sharing the parenting load fairly."

We need a system for diagramming the "level" of beliefs and values. NLP has frequently utilized a map called, "Logical Levels" for this purpose.

Logical Levels

Logical levels were first explored (to my knowledge) by Gregory Bateson. Robert Dilts later expanded upon his model. These people and others have postulated that there are several "levels" to our logical processes. The "Logical Levels" frequently distinguished are the **Environments** in which we operate, our **Behaviors**, our **Capabilities**, **Beliefs**, **Identity**, and the **Source** of our Identity – or that greater whole of which we are a part - whatever we call that. People often talk about responding to things on different "levels." For instance, someone might say that some experience was negative on one level, but positive on another level. In our brain structure, our language, and our perceptual systems there are natural hierarchies or levels of experience. One purpose of each level is to organize and control the information on the level below it. Changing something on an upper level would necessarily change things on the lower levels. However; changing something on a lower level could - but might not necessarily - affect the upper levels.

The Environment level involves the specific external conditions and contexts in which our Behavior takes place. I function in an office environment. Living in the Chicago area, I must often function in a traffic environment. Different environments and contexts require different Behaviors. I have a huge variety of Behaviors that I must do during a day. I am Capable of a large number of different Behaviors. Which Capabilities I choose to develop is guided by the next higher level, my Beliefs and Values. I must make my Beliefs and Values fit into a larger structure of who I am as a person, or my Identity. And my Identity arises out of who or what I think I am in relation to the larger whole –whatever we want to call that greater whole – Source, God, Light, whatever.

Environmental factors determine the external opportunities or limitations with which a person has to contend. You find out the environment by asking **"Where" and "When" questions.** It is "socially superficial" but also safe to ask people questions like, "Where do you work?" or "When did that happen?" Many therapists find benefit when they clarify, "Where in your life is this a problem for you?"

Behavior is made up of the specific actions or reactions enacted within an environment. You find out about behavior by asking **"What" and/or action questions.** "What did you do in response to that?" "What did you think was going to happen?" "What will you do about that?"

Capabilities are behavioral actions, sequences, plans, and strategies. You find out these things by asking **"How" questions.** Questions like, "How are you going to deal with that?" or, "How do you plan on doing this?" ask about plans and strategies.

You find out about beliefs and values by asking about beliefs and values! If you use the **"Why" question,** you will make people defensive. Instead, ask, **"What is important to you in this context?" or, "What is important to you about that?"** One of the reasons beliefs are so important is that they provide the motivation and permission that supports us in developing specific capabilities. If I believe I can go to school and get a degree, I am much more likely to apply to a school than if I don't believe I have that ability. If I believe a certain plan of action might work, I am much more likely to invest time and energy in enacting the plan.

Identity factors determine overall purpose (mission) and shape beliefs and values by helping to create a coherent sense of self. To find out about identity level issues, ask, "What kind of a person are you that you…" These answer the abstract question, **"Who am I?"** Whenever people tell you something really positive that they do or believe, you could ask them, "So what kind of person are you that you believe/do that?" This can help to solidify a positive sense of identity.

Source refers to, "a sense of being part of a much vaster system" than our own Identity, including family, community/profession, planet, universe, God. These are generally questions about a person's religion or personal philosophy.

These levels are most frequently presented as a triangle:

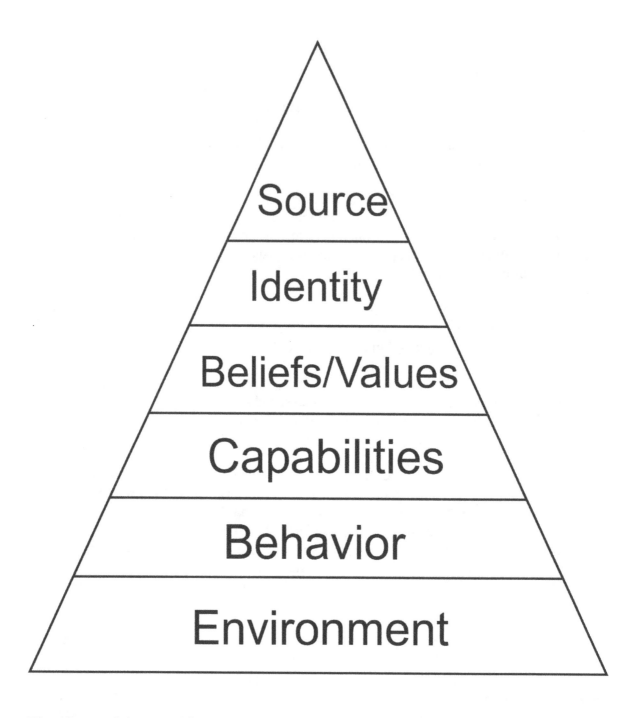

Einstein stated that a problem couldn't be solved at the same level as its creation. So, in order to make a change, we need to shift the logical level to one that has a broader or higher level of leverage than the one at which we identify the problem. For example, alcoholics and other addicted people often make their first attempts at change by moving out of the areas in which they currently use (Environment). This alone doesn't work because the issues they are addressing are also Behavioral, Capability, Belief, and Identity issues. Alcoholics Anonymous helps people instead start at the Source level to make changes.

When you make belief changes, you can leverage the change by going to a higher-level belief or value. You do this by strategically using sleight-of-mouth patterns and presuppositions, which are discussed later in this book. Once the shift is made, you work on lower levels to assure that the change generalizes out into the real world and gets implemented in their life.

Beliefs are Recursive Evaluations

One of the things that make mapping beliefs even more interesting is that beliefs occur at each of the logical levels. We have beliefs about our environment (How clean should my apartment be kept?), beliefs about our behavior (Do I want to behave like other people?), beliefs about our capabilities (I could go to college and get a better job), beliefs about our beliefs (My religion is THE right one), beliefs about our identity (I AM a nice person, I don't care what anybody says!) and beliefs about the Source level (There is a Source or there isn't, or maybe it cares about me as an individual, or it doesn't…). The point is, beliefs happen all the time, at all levels. As we learn how to change belief structures, we need to be careful to change beliefs at the proper logical level.

We often utilize the logical levels map by conversationally helping the client to change logical levels. When we ask the questions from the outcome template, asking the question, "What's important about that?" asks for a value to be stated in the response. We can invite a person to comment about identity issues by saying, "What kind of person are you, that you have these beliefs and values?" We can ask about capabilities a person has, and about behaviors they do.

Often we try to get the person to move "up" the logical levels when we want to:
- Create more motivation
- Uncover an outcome that is more agreeable to the listener
- Uncover a strategy that is more practical or achievable

We often try to get the person to move "down" the logical levels when we want to:
- Implement a specific plan of action
- Assure application of a generalization
- Change a course of action previously used

Moving up the logical levels is utilized when we ask for meta-outcomes. If you ask an employee what is important about a project they are working on, they may say, "I have to keep my boss happy." If you ask what is important about keeping their boss happy, they may reply, "I'd like to keep my job, and keeping the boss happy lets me keep my job." By asking again, what is important about that, they might reply, "I keep my job so I can feed my family, I feed my family so I can be a good parent, I want to be a good parent so I can feel good about myself." Suddenly, the simple project the person was working on "just to keep their boss happy" fits in with keeping their family satisfied and being a good parent. Often people lose this "larger perspective" when they experience frustration at a lower logical level, and helping them to shift upward helps them to re-evaluate the importance and value of an activity.

Moving down the logical levels is a way of making sure that shifts and changes in values get reflected in changes in the outer world and environment. When we help people reframe ideas, or re-think about their situation, we need to make sure those shifts get put into action by asking about how they will change their behavior and environment to allow for the expression of the new internal thinking or state.

Often when a person is "vaguely unhappy" it is because what they are doing in their behavior and environment is not supporting their capabilities and beliefs. They often need to travel up the logical levels, clarify their own values and beliefs, and then travel down the logical levels to review how they are implementing their values and beliefs in their daily life.

Beliefs Lead to States

The 4th Component of a Belief

While beliefs are made up of evidence, labels and frames, the end result of fulfilling the evidence and "attaining" the label is always a state. If solving problems were as easy as finding the list of criteria, it could all easily be taken over by computers. But, what people really want when they start seeking to improve is to attain some state that they do not currently feel is possible for them. People organize their lives into beliefs and evidence so that they have a series of steps and processes that will lead them to some highly desired state.

For example, Mr. Smith is working to make more money so he can "provide a good home for my family." If he is asked the right questions, he will give you his evidence for a "good home for his family." But the final result of providing this good home will be his enjoyment of a state when he believes; "I am a good provider for my family." This "state" is part of his meta-outcome, and in fact is the motivation to acquire the evidence. Where did he get this silly belief? From his father - an authority - who told him that the "...real measure of a man was if he could provide a good home for his family." Unfortunately, Dad did not spell out the evidence for "a good home" clearly, and so Mr. Smith is doing his best to fill in the blanks. He is working two jobs to make extra money. He is also adopting some of his wife's criteria in order to keep his marriage functional.

We can diagram this as follows:

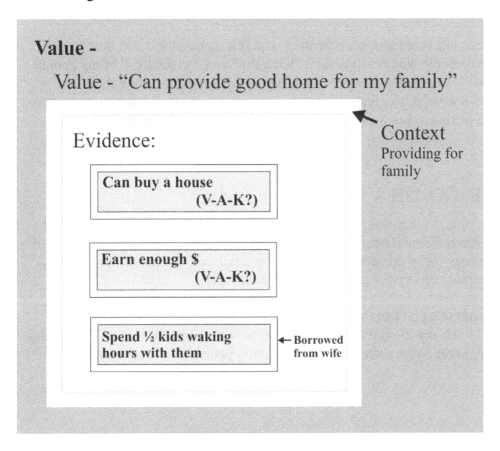

While we structure our lives in nests and sequences of beliefs and evidence, we use these structures to achieve particular states. It is possible to simply ask the person, "So if you can provide for your family in just the way you want to, how will you be feeling?" The person does not need to verbally answer – simply look for the non-verbal shifts that tell you their state has changed, and then anchor that shift with a smile, with a word/label, or with a gesture. This is also one tiny aspect of an incredible technique called, "Core Transformation," developed by Dr. Connirae Andreas.

People are always evaluating the world. We always think of ideas and compare them to other ideas, or compare them to other things. We must be able to make sense out of the world, so we impose structures onto the world. Whenever an event happens in the world, we have to categorize that input is an instance or example of something. It doesn't change the world, but it makes us more able to navigate through it and get what we want and need.

The bottom line is, you don't just ask about ideas – you ask about ideas and feelings! You ask about beliefs and values to show honoring of how the other individual has structured their world. This builds very deep rapport. Then, after you have honored their structure, you can invite them to simply experience the state that structure was designed to allow them to experience. By anchoring the state, you then pair that state with the changes that they have told you they want, and they will be more motivated to take steps and make changes, because you "strengthen" the "connection" of their belief about those particular steps leading to their outcome.

As you practice to become more and more familiar with this material and continue to elicit belief structures from people, you begin to do it "naturally" and "on the fly." Many people have commented that it takes some practice to master the "diagramming" of beliefs and values, but once it is learned it becomes absolutely "automatic" in a wide variety of contexts. It is a useful skill in getting to know people, and in increasing your ability to influence others.

BEFORE WE GO ON –

You are about to study influential language so let's pose a question... Why do you suppose the therapeutic question, "Why do you think your life is a failure?" is one of the most horrible, most damaging things you can say to a human being?

If you haven't figured out a good answer by the end of the next section, try this – Ask yourself, "Why do I think my life is a failure?" and see how it makes YOU feel! (If you did slip into feeling bad, anchor your internal state to enjoying yourself before proceeding.)

The Two Types of Beliefs

There are two basic types of beliefs:

1. Cause-Effects (C-E beliefs)
2. Complex Equivalences (CEq beliefs)

Cause-Effect beliefs are beliefs about sequences and things that "make" each other happen. When people say, "If I go to school, I will make more money," they are telling you they believe there is a cause-effect linkage between the event of going to school and the event of making more money.

Complex Equivalences are really VERY SIMPLE equivalences. I do not understand why they were named complex, when in fact they are incredibly simple equivalences. When a person says, "My husband spending time with the kids and giving me a certain look means he is a good husband," she has handed you the complex equivalence for that belief. Complex equivalence means simply, "this event/behavior = (equals) this meaning."

While a person may have beliefs of both types, people will have a "preference" and they will build most of their belief structures out of one of these two types of beliefs.

This is one of the first distinctions taught to NLP students about beliefs. There is a lot of complicated material based on trying to determine if a person has a C-E belief system, or a primarily CEq belief structure. There are really two very simple ways to tell which a person uses more frequently.

1. If they keep using words like, "makes, causes, 'and then', 'so then...'" they are building mostly C-E beliefs. They talk in terms of procedures, steps and causes.

2. If they keep talking about what things "mean," use a lot of abstractions in their evidence, or have several levels of "nesting" in their beliefs, they are building mostly CEq beliefs.

In their non-verbal behavior, people who build C-E beliefs will tend to gesture with their hand in a "left-to-right" gesture. They will literally "point" on their timeline to events following one another. They will say, "Well that (point to location 1) makes you do (point to location 2, to their right of location 1) that..." They will tend to use cause-effect statements in their arguments.

People who build mostly CEq beliefs will often gesture in more vertical arrangements. They will say, "Well that (point to location 1) means you are/can (point to location 2, which will be ABOVE location 1) have/get..." They will spend time "relating" to you and telling you how "this means that," and will tend to use more nominalizations or abstractions.

Section 4: Structures for Belief Systems

Beliefs and Time

Beliefs connect to what is present in our world in the present moment, what was present in the past, and guide what we think will be present in the future. So beliefs actually impact our sense of time, and how we experience time also impacts how we build belief structures.

Everyone experiences a sense of time differently. But, as usual, there are ways to categorize how people experience time.

The "In-Time Person"

People who have what is called "in-time orientation" tend to be more in touch with their feelings, or, as they say in NLP, more "associated." They tend to get "lost in time." They go to the grocery store with the intent of going for a few minutes, and they get lost in the experience. They are more often late, because they got lost in time or projects and simply forgot to look up at the clock. In-time people get a bit more emotional and worked-up when they tell you about an experience they had, because they often re-live events when they describe them to another person. It may take them a while to "get into it," but when they get there, they are re-living it. They tend to be more focused on the present, on how they are feeling, and they use instinct and intuition more frequently. They have strong emotional reactions to events around them. They tend to "immerse" themselves in projects and people. They also have a timeline that has their past behind them, and their future in front of them.

The "Through-Time Person"

The through-time person tends to be more intellectual, more emotionally "aloof," more emotionally calculating and less enthusiastic. I am not implying they have this as a problem, they are just likely to be less emotionally charged. They may become enthused about things, but it takes longer, and they feel it less intensely. They are more what is called in NLP, "disassociated." They are less in touch with their own feelings, are more likely to be timely for appointments and meetings. They are good at planning and procedures. They are likely to have more medical problems, because they are often "out of touch" with their body, and don't notice tiny, subtle body signals. Rather than getting "enthused, " they are more likely to commit to a plan based on believing it will work, rather than getting excited and relying on "raw motivation" to go with a plan. This makes them stick to a task a little easier than the in-time person, because they don't rely on the constant motivation. They most often have a timeline that stretches their past out on the left, and their future on their right side.

The "Between-Time Person"

The between-time person goes back and forth from in-time and through-time. They easily "re-live" experiences and become immersed in them. They then step "out" of the experience, and go back to being somewhat disassociated. They are always comparing one experience to another experience that has some similarity to the first experience. They "hop back and forth" between experiences – often cued by feelings. If you ask an in-time person about things that make them happy, and they will tend to pick one event or idea and stay there for a while. If you ask a through-time person about things that make them happy, they will not have much emotional reaction, but will instead go through their experiences and calmly report the ones that have made them happy. The between-time person will use the happy feeling as a "lead" and will quickly search their timeline and re-live a number of different experiences they categorize as happy, and very likely show more emotion than a through-time person. These people often do extremely well in school, because they are always comparing one idea to another "similar" idea. Between time people easily shift their timelines from through-time to in-time in a split second.

The Three Types of Belief Structures

One dictionary defines a belief as, "...something accepted as true, what one believes." 1 [Oxford American Dictionary, Heald Colleges Edition, © 1980, Avon Books, New York, NY]
Another dictionary defines belief as, "a state or habit of mind in which trust or confidence is placed in some person or thing." It goes on to say that the idea is related to faith, credence, and credit. 2 [Webster's New Collegiate Dictionary, © 1976, G. & C. Mirriam Co., Springfield, Massachusetts, pg. 101]

Obviously these are very different definitions. I believe it is because they are describing one or another of the three basic types of belief structures that people use in the world. The first definition is about "**rules.**" The second definition refers to **states**, and also to **sequences**.

The first definition treats a belief as a "thing" by using the word "something." This "thing" or object is then either accepted as true or not true. When these "things" reach the status of true, they are called "beliefs." So we have a sort of "sheep and goats" system for these "things." (By the way, did you automatically assume that true=sheep and false=goats? Why not true=goats and false=sheep?? Remember that thing about prejudice?) However, we are given no inkling of how these things achieve the status of "true." How do we tell "sheep" beliefs from "goat" beliefs? And what if I get a "goat-in-sheep's-clothing" belief? We have to know our criteria for sheep and goat beliefs in order to have this type of a "rule-based" belief structure. Evidence is very important in **rule-based belief structures.** These people use raw evidence, and build their own conclusions from this evidence. Rule-based belief structures are sensitive to redefining and content reframing, where the same evidence is re-interpreted, and the rule changes as a result of "allowing" for another possible meaning. This type of belief structure is often associated with through-time people. Little emotion is attached to belief – they are "simply facts." They tend to have fairly simple belief structures.

In the second definition, belief is a "state or habit of mind..." I find this a really interesting idea, because it does not even talk about the process of "being accepted as true." It simply refers to a particular "cocktail" of brain chemicals that apparently our brain regularly or frequently mixes for us. After all, it is referred to as a "habit of mind." As if my mind has a series of functions and habits in a daily schedule like, "Brush your teeth, stand upright, and think of something you have confidence in as a fact every few minutes, so I can feel confident and trust the world is consistent." I believe that we actually do exactly this. I think we create the state of "it's true" just so we can feel confident about how to function in the world. This is an example of a **"state-based" belief system**. Ideas have to "feel really certain and right" to be accepted as facts in state-based belief structures. This type of belief structure is often associated with in-time people. They are more in touch with their internal states and emotions, rather than being "semi-numb" like many more intellectual people. State-based belief systems are sensitive to anchoring and "inducing doubt."

The second definition then goes on to say trust or confidence is placed IN some person or thing. This statement is thus using the metaphor of a person or thing as a CONTAINER, and also some FLUID or SUBSTANCE (believable-ness) is placed INTO this container. In this type of belief structure, the container often itself becomes "imbued with the quality" of the substance it contains. Sometimes, "containers" are believed to also be able to "bestow" the quality (in this case "believable-ness") on other things/containers/beliefs, by "granting the fluid." This is how an expert bestows "believableness" upon a belief they give us. It is smothered in "truth syrup," which it earned after some process. We relate the feeling of truth to beliefs sometimes just because we heard them from someone we trust, read them from a source, or were led to them by someone logically. This is an example of a **"process-based" belief system.** This person must reason their way from the evidence to a generalization themselves (or be led by another) in order to accept something as a fact. They like to run their convincer strategy. In their language, they use a lot of generalizations and abstractions. They are sensitive to shifts that involve "playing" higher-level beliefs "against" lower level beliefs, or meaning shifts. This type of belief structure is often associated with between-time people.

And yes, we all use all three of these. However, we will have a preference for how we build beliefs within a particular domain or area of our life.

Frames, Chunk Size and Scope

We have already talked about beliefs and frames. We can define a frame as the currently highlighted context of attention. Within any context or frame, certain ideas or things will be recognized as "members of a frame." Previously I used the example of using music as a frame. When I am having a conversation with my friend Melodie about music, I know that she studied music at the same school I did, and that we have many, many similar elements that we recognize as members of the frame, "music." If I talk with her about "Bach music I have been enjoying lately," she would probably ask me which of his music I was enjoying – Two-part inventions for the keyboard? Orchestral works? Vocal music he wrote? For most people, I could just say, "I have been enjoying Bach's music lately." And they would just sort of say, "Ok, sure." But Melodie knows more specific information about Bach music, and if I just said to her, "I have been enjoying Bach's music lately," this would be a large chunk size for her, and she would invite me to be more specific.

Chunking is a very interesting phenomenon in psychology. If we take the letters:

TH-EDO-GSA-WT-HEC-AT and try to learn or memorize them, it could be quite a hassle. But if we instead look at the letters and realize they spell out, "The dog saw the cat," memorizing them becomes incredibly easy! Instead of learning a sequence of random letters, we have "chunked" them into words, and now instead of having to remember 15 letters, we only have to remember 1 sentence. In the context of beliefs, chunk size refers to how "much" (or what "size" experience) is "sliced off" and labeled as an example of something. It has to do with the level of detail at which the person is focused. While many people would accept "Bach's music" as an element, my friend Melodie would think that was a very large chunk, and would want more detail.

Chunking is also a very important part of building prejudice. If we ascribe certain qualities to people of a certain race (a huge "chunk" of the population), we are not likely to allow for counter-examples, because that would force us to re-build our maps and add more detail. That would mean we would have to think and "work" on adjusting our beliefs, and most people don't just decide to do that on a whim. We need multiple examples, or examples over time, or one very "strong" counter-example in order to really change beliefs.

One of my favorite examples of this has nothing to do with race – but is a different kind of prejudice. I live in the Chicago area. A very common prejudice here is that people who have a southern accent are stupid. I have often been in business meetings where a speaker has what I refer to as "a twang" – meaning, a southern accent. As a musician, I absolutely LOVE accents and "twangs." I delight in hearing the differences in tonality people use in pronouncing a word. But I often see "northerners" rolling their eyes, smiling at each other, or even all-out mocking a person, simply because they have an accent. Even if the speaker is articulate, accurate, clear and intelligent, they will have to prove this clearly and repeatedly to overcome the prejudice in that "northerner" room. And even if they establish themselves as an exception or counter-example to this "Southerners are stupid" prejudice, the very next person speaking with such an accent will still have to prove himself or herself as intelligent. If we meet three or four such "intelligent southerners," we are more likely to form a belief that, "Southern people from that particular **company** are intelligent," rather than actually change our prejudice about the larger group.

Another common prejudice is toward fat people. (I mean, "gravitationally challenged" individuals!) Fat people are often thought of as lazy and less intelligent. This is a very strong prejudice in American culture, and while we all know of exceptions, the prejudice still tends to hold for the larger group. (Larger group meaning the frame "fat people," not just the "fatter of the fat people.")

On the logical levels diagram, chunk size is "horizontal." It refers to how many elements are contained in a frame, and the "size" of the elements in that frame.

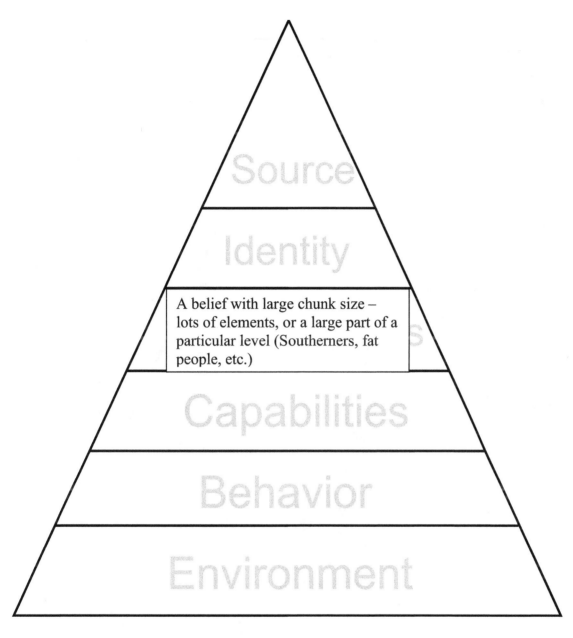

A belief with large chunk size – lots of elements, or a large part of a particular level (Southerners, fat people, etc.)

There is another quality of beliefs that is vertical – called, "Scope."

Of all the qualities of beliefs, the most poorly defined in NLP appears to be the concept of "scope." Scope refers to the "pervasiveness" of an idea or a belief. It has to do with how many logical levels or domains contain or are influenced by a particular belief. It has to do with how "vertical" or "generalizable" a particular belief or value is.

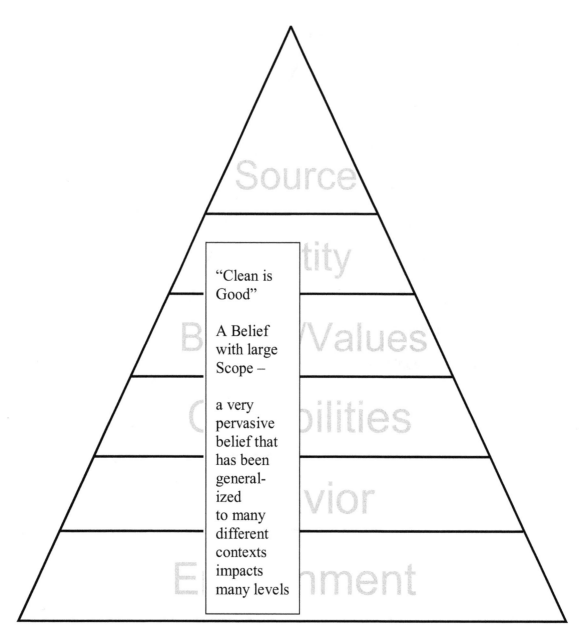

For example, I may believe it is very important to be clean. This belief could influence my behavior and my other beliefs in a variety of ways. Using the logical levels model, I may believe it is important to maintain a clean **environment**. The "chunk size" of this belief may include things like washing my body, vacuuming my house, keeping the kitchen clear of food particles and dirty dishes, and keeping my car clean. Or, the "chunk size" of this belief might include recycling paper and plastic, cleaning the parking lot of my apartment building, or belonging to several environmental activist groups. If I greatly value the **behavior** of vacuuming, washing the dishes, and picking up garbage, then the belief "It is important to be clean" is widening in scope to include "clean-oriented behaviors." If I learn about the latest technology in killing germs and use it in my kitchen, the scope of the belief is now climbing "up" the logical levels model to include **capabilities** being directed toward "being clean." If I truly **value** being clean, I may work to "push" this value onto others, including my children. If I think I am a "Clean Person" (**identity** level), I may make cleaning my life goal, and open a cleaning service. And finally, I may truly and fully believe that "Cleanliness is next to Godliness" and therefore, "It is important to be clean" would be a belief that had incredible and pervasive scope within all the logical levels of my belief system.

In contrast, I may have "Be clean" as a very "large scope" belief that impacts each of the logical levels, however, I may only be referring to "clean thoughts" (small chunk size). I may never think bad things about people because that would be against my **religion**, would violate my **values**, and I am **capable** of "finding good" in any person. And my **behavior** might never show disfavor for people, no matter where I am (**environment**) – But I may live in an absolute filth pit in my home – all the while, still proposing that "keeping clean" is very important in my life. This belief would be wide in scope, but have very small chunk size.

In the model we use to diagram beliefs, scope and chunk size are not utilized or diagrammed. As you begin to use language patterns to influence belief structures, scope and chunk size begin to become more important.

Section 5: Changing Beliefs Using NLP Models

Changing Beliefs Using NLP Models

Honesty and Ethics

If you work with belief shifting, you need to be ethical and honest in your work. Asking strategic questions of your clients does most of the shifting. When you ask and answer questions, you help to build their confidence in you as an expert. Also, as an expert, the information you give to your client or customer will be given a "special status" called, "factual, truthful, believable" information. As an expert, and as a person in an assisting role, you must be very careful to only give your client truthful information. It is perfectly acceptable to say, "I don't know." This is because your "information" is still reliable – you have informed the person that you do not know the answer. But if you instead falsify information, your client will detect it unconsciously in your communication. While we utilize the tools of ethical influence to assist others in accepting opinions and ideas, you never want to use these tools to disguise or distort facts. This would destroy the trust and rapport that is so vital to any beneficial interaction.

The most important aspect of changing beliefs is not how to CHANGE a belief, but what target belief to shift the belief INTO in its place! When you change a belief, you leave a "void," and that void must be filled in by another belief. (Notice the underlying metaphor of containers in those last statements?) In other words, if you simply change a belief, you never know how that change will impact the larger system – the person! This is the notion in NLP of ecology – how does this change impact the larger system of the person and their environment. If you simply change a belief, sometimes you can disrupt a very essential belief in the person's belief structure. This can have very powerful positive or negative effects.

I remember one of my NLP instructors (Robert McDonald) taking a short time-out from teaching belief change processes to literally BEG the class, "Please, do not mess with people's religious beliefs." I will always remember from how deeply inside his heart that request came, and how sincerely he meant it. The true test of that came literally knocking on my door one day. A certain "door to door" church group had built a new church near my home, and the fourth group of evangelists came knocking on my door in their never-ending attempt to convert me. Irritated by their ignoring of my polite and repeated "No thank you," I invited them in with less-than-kind intentions, and suddenly remembered my NLP instructor and his plea for ecology. I looked at the visitors and said, "I have to tell you… I have studied a lot of hypnosis, and my specialty is changing people's beliefs conversationally. If you have come here to convert me, I confess, I will be equally active in trying to un-convert you." They nearly fell over each other running out the door! (Note: Some people have judged me as a "bad person" for even thinking of that. Two important points: 1.) I didn't actually DO it! I stopped myself. 2.) I WARNED the people overtly, and they decided to leave. I also would have considered it unethical to do covert belief change work with them, and so I did not do that.)

When you change a belief, it is vital to have a target belief. The safest beliefs to add are beliefs about capabilities. I learned (from Steve Andreas) that the only exception to this rule is the belief, "I am a worthwhile person." That belief is at the identity level, and is a HUGE shift for people who don't already have it in their thinking. If it does disrupt their world or their life, it is generally in very positive directions. It may significantly disrupt their life – for example, an abused spouse may decide they are no longer going to tolerate abuse from their spouse – but in the larger scheme of things, it would still be a positive change.

If you change a person's belief to, "I am a professional chiropractor" (identity level), they may go out and begin adjusting people's necks and backs without the proper training – all the while feeling perfectly comfortable doing such procedures without really knowing all of the intricacies of such a process. If instead you change their belief to, "I can BECOME a professional chiropractor," you help to increase their motivation for such training and education without having them "jump the gun." In my own brain, I have experimented incessantly with changing my own beliefs. I once decided to add the belief, "I can do anything!" It felt really good! I felt really competent and capable… I needed to go to the grocery store, so I got in the car to go. I got to the end of the driveway, and stopped. I realized I had just backed the car up rapidly without ever looking behind me, checking for traffic, or otherwise allowing for some other events in the outside world. I quickly changed the belief to, "I can LEARN to do anything I want to learn to do" and just as quickly resumed doing things like looking both ways before I pulled into traffic! This is also an example of the unconscious mind treating the "languaging" of the new belief as literal – "I can DO ANYTHIING. No consequences. No training needed. Just, I can, because I believe it." Really NOT a very useful belief! And yes, many people appear to have this belief.

You need to spend time with a client, developing a target belief, working with objections to different beliefs, and otherwise "tailoring" a new belief for them. If you don't know how to do this sort of thing, please don't change people's beliefs! If you want to learn how to do this sort of thing well, you may wish to study Human Animal Behavior Trainingsm via Expanding Enterprises, Inc. You will find HABTsm runs circles around "just" NLP training in making shifts effective and efficient. Again, if you are not willing to put that much time and effort into learning to do this process safely and effectively, please pick another hobby!

Well-Formedness Conditions for Beliefs

It is my hope that you have at least questioned or wondered about, "What kinds of beliefs would be good or bad for people to have? Certainly, believing, "Everything is wonderful" sounds great, but if one loses the negative reaction to things like torture and genocide, that is not very useful as a citizen of the world. So, one guideline is to AVOID changing beliefs to new beliefs of enormous scope, as it is very difficult to predict the impact such beliefs would create.

Instead, when creating the new belief, keep the following suggestions in mind:
- Phrase it as an ability or capability, or future direction. ("I can LEARN to…" or, "I can allow myself to…" of, "I can let go of…"
- Make sure the change is initiated, controlled and evaluated by Self, not someone else. (Make sure they are changing in a way THEY want to change, not so that they will live up to another's expectations and get their approval.)

- Beliefs about themselves are easier to adopt that new beliefs about the world
- Phrase the belief in a comfortable, positive and motivating way

Take some time to "craft" a belief statement, and involve the other person in that careful wording.

Believing and States

The second definition of beliefs listed in this book included the phrase, "…a STATE or habit of mind…" Many times we believe something because of the state we are in when we discover an idea. This is especially true for people with state-based belief structures. This quickly becomes a circular definition: Which came first - the state? Or the believing? Rather than chase our tails in an attempt to explain that, I will simply claim that either can actually come first.

If I am in the presence of an expert (that is, I believe they are an expert!) who is talking about a topic, I tend to be "predisposed" to believe what they tell me. This means I have an internal state of "true," and everything they say will be filtered through this state. This is one of the ways experts quickly build beliefs. (The opposite can also happen – I can go to hear someone speak, and can be a "hostile listener" – defended and ready to disagree with everything they say, no matter how truthful or accurate it may be.)

If I am paying attention to the expert's talk, and I strongly disagree with something the expert says, I might quickly shift out of the state of "true" and into a state of "not believing." If I then agree with the next several points the speaker says, I may return to an internal state of "true." However, if I am not paying attention, or I totally trust (intense state of "true") the expert, I may not allow myself to go into a state of "not believing." I may simply accept what they say without critically or fully examining the information. This is particularly true when a close-knit group or large portion of society strongly supports what the expert is telling me. This "keeping the audience agreeing" is one factor in how Hitler got some pretty bizarre beliefs into people early in this century, how cult leaders get their bizarre beliefs into "followers," and how a good convincing public speaker gets you to go along with their speech. They deliberately keep you in a state of "true" as strongly as possible, and carefully mix the obvious with the new ideas to try to slip ideas in while you are in a "state of true." Television advertisers are also using this process more and more frequently. They start by asking you two or three questions to which the obvious answer is "yes," and then they ask you if you want to buy their product. They are hoping you will keep your "true" or "agreeing" state as they ask the next question. This is also how good NLP practitioners develop effective use of basic hypnotic language patterns.

If you use linkages and other linguistic methods to connect ideas together, you can get the listener into a state of "true" while you add more ideas to the content of your phrase. I teach this method in trainings, and I call it "Yupping Your Client." You simply ask them several questions that they will obviously agree with, and then use language patterns to add a "questionable idea." You must be VERY careful to not produce a state of "not believing" when you attempt to "yup" your listener. Such changes are made in little steps by shifting ideas into conversations while the person is in a state of "true." And it usually works best to do two "trues" followed by a "questionable." People often chunk information into groups of three ideas. More about that later…

Our emotional state has significant impact on our "impressionability." Several different methods of influencing a person into an emotional state of greater "impressionability" are discussed in Robert Cialdini's book, "Influence," and Richard Brodie's book, "Virus of the Mind." Both these authors point to the evolving science of influence and the increasing precision with which we wield such skills. I prefer to distinguish between using such skills to obtain your own outcome (unethical influence) and using the same skills to help others attain THEIR outcomes and goals (Creative Influence - the name of one of my advanced HABTsm courses).

One emotional state that significantly influences beliefs is the state of "important." We can have unimportant and insignificant beliefs, and we can have beliefs that influence and impact nearly ALL of our other beliefs. Many people have religious beliefs for which they would gladly die. I find it absolutely fascinating that people are literally willing to give up their lives for things that exist only as abstractions and mental constructs. I do not wish to diminish the importance of any particular beliefs with that statement! I am merely making an observation about the "power" of beliefs in our lives. Especially the power of beliefs we deem important. Beliefs that have enormous scope are automatically important beliefs.

Changing Beliefs Using Sequenced Anchoring

Even if you are already a licensed clinician or therapist, if you intend to utilize the techniques in this book it is highly recommended that you obtain certification and HABTsm training in applying models and techniques of NLP before simply attempting any belief change processes with a person. You would want to study and master some techniques for distinguishing and creating shifts in others at lower logical levels, and be confident in your ability to do this before attempting to change a client's beliefs. If you are a traditional therapist with no HABTsm or NLP training and think you understand what was just said, then you have just demonstrated that you do not understand this well enough to know how completely different it is than the standard methods and models of treatment.

Note about using these techniques: If you are not a therapist, please stop and ask yourself why you are trying to change someone's beliefs. If you are not a licensed mental health treatment provider, it is very likely that you should NOT be attempting such a thing in the first place. If you insist on using such techniques, please be willing to get the proper training so that you can "Do no harm" by confusing the steps or distinctions necessary to complete the process effectively. Until you understand the importance of ecology, the requirement of the client participating in the development of their belief, the ways of testing for objections and how to "adjust" different techniques, it is not recommended that you simply attempt to follow a "recipe" that uses ingredients you might not fully know how to work with and adjust as needed. Ask any chemist how dangerous that can be.

Anchoring-Based NLP Techniques

Some of the most incredibly powerful interventions and changes you can make are accomplished by utilizing what seem like very small, very slight, and yet very significant shifts you can easily lead a person through – even covertly during a conversation. This will become clearer as you learn how to apply anchoring in more strategic and specific ways. You can help people to gather and generate resources in powerful ways that can support them in making the changes they want in their life.

By very carefully sequencing and anchoring a series of states, we can offer people the opportunity to more consciously choose the things they wish to believe about themselves and the world.

This technique requires:
1. A belief the person would **like** to believe about themselves, but they are not completely sure is true.
   a. There are a lot of ecology checks to go through in making this functional and balanced for the individual.

Component States to Anchor for Belief Change

This is diagrammed on the next pages. Use a sheet of paper for each square, and write what is written in the squares in the diagram onto the papers. You will be having the person literally stepping on the papers and walking through them as a path or sequence of states.

The overall sequence of states is as follows:

1. Meta-position A

2. Limiting belief about self – How does it feel to believe this?
3. Uncertainty, leaning toward doubt. (Something you think might be true, but you tend to think it is not true.)
4. "I used to believe this." – Museum of Old Beliefs – Some old belief that you know is no longer true at all. (Magical childhood thinking is often useful.)

5. Meta-position B

6. I neither believe nor doubt this – an idea – Target belief (State of balanced, "Maybe, maybe not."
7. I am open to believing this –Uncertainty but leaning toward believing
8. This is ABSOLUTELY, CERTAINLY true – Absolutely certain.

AFTER you have gone through, anchoring each of the states to each space, you go through, skipping the stars – the "Mini-Meta-Positions" – and walk from paper to paper, state to state, directly.

9. Then bring the newly installed belief from the space of "Certainty" over into space #2 – "Limiting belief about self" previous location. You want the new/target belief to occupy the "same space" as the old belief used to, and check the ecology of it being in the exact same location. Adjust the belief as needed.

All of which makes much more sense as a diagram or set of dance steps on the floor, which is shown on the next page::

Changing Beliefs by Sequenced Anchors

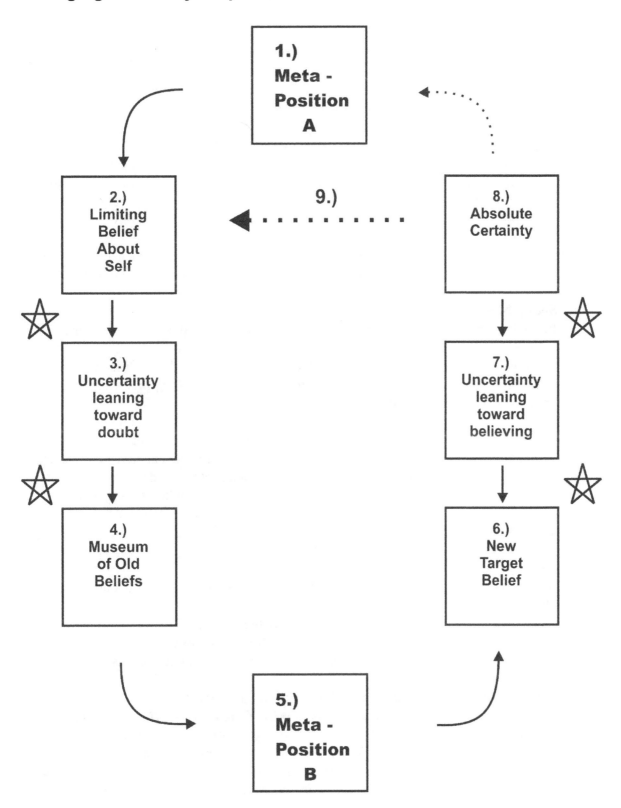

Instructions: Changing Beliefs by Sequenced Anchors - Script
(Done in trios, A, B and C. 30 mins each.)

> Have a completed and ecological target belief crafted before you continue with this exercise.
>
> Have A write down this "approved" new belief about self on a piece of paper, and put it in their pocket or hang on to it.

You first setup each of the spaces (the papers on the floor) with a specific state related to believing. By doing this, each page becomes an anchor. You will guide the person through the process twice – once to anchor a state to each of the pieces of paper. On the first walk through, you will have the person repeatedly stepping off/out of the sequence of papers and on to the star positions. You will not use the star positions the second time through.

What follows is a script of invitations for setting up the desired state in each space. We invite you to add your own as well – utilizing any language patterns you may already know.

1. **Set up Meta-Position A:**
    Invite the person into Observer/Meta Position, and have them stand on the paper on the floor marked, "Meta-Position A. <u>AS</u> they step onto the spot, say, ***"Don't just do this mentally. Stand physically on that space, and show me 'The Observer' mode with your posture. Go, "hmmm…' as an observer, overlooking this whole process with mild, observer curiosity."***

    Remember – The first time you take them through this, you set up each of the papers as an anchor for the state written on it. (After they step off the paper, you distract the person or break their state, so they can access a "clean" state for each page.) To step off of the path, have the person step onto the "star positions when setting up the anchors," and use the star positions as mini-meta positions while they access the appropriate state for the next paper/step.

2. **Set up Limiting Belief about Self:**
    Invite A to look over at the spot marked, "Limiting Belief about Self." and as an observer, just look at it. Notice and align any reactions.
    a. Have A step into and speak the limiting belief FROM THAT SPACE.
    b. **"Just notice what it feels like to have that belief in that space, and notice how long it has been in place. How does it feel to believe this?"**

3. **Break State, Then Set up Uncertainty Leaning Toward Doubt:**
    "Now step OFF the papers, and step BETWEEN the Limiting Belief about Self page (shown as a star on the diagram,) ***and just go again into 'Observer' – just looking at this with curiosity. Think about the next state – and look at the paper for, "Uncertainty leaning toward doubt.' What is something you believe, but you also kind of doubt? And your leaning is toward thinking it is not so true…"***

a. As A accesses such a belief, have them step onto paper marked, "Uncertainty leaning toward doubt." Again ask them to describe what it feels like to believe something, but lean toward doubting it.

4. **Break, Then Set up Museum of Old Beliefs:**
"Now step OFF the papers again, and step BETWEEN the Uncertainty leaning toward doubt page (shown as a star on the diagram) *and just go again into 'Observer' – just looking at this with curiosity. Think about the next state – and look at the paper for, "Museum of Old Beliefs – which is something you used to believe, but now you know it is definitely not true.' What is something you believed, maybe as a kid, but now know is incorrect, and maybe it was even a little silly?"*
   a. When A accesses such a belief, have them step on to the paper marked, "Museum of Old Beliefs." Get several. Honor old beliefs – made sense then.

5. **Break and Set up Meta-Position B**:
"Now just step forward into the spot marked, "Meta-Position B.' Look again as an observer overlooking this mildly interesting process."

6. **Set up Target Belief:**
Have a target belief completely written out, as a target belief. Have the person write it out, and **have them step into this space and read it to you** from this space on the floor. Just notice their reactions.

7. **Break, Then Set up Uncertainty Leaning Toward Believing:**
"Step off the papers (onto a mini-observer/star location) *and access a specific belief that is something that feels uncertain, but you lean toward believing it. Any kinds of belief you believe, and you may not be 100% sure of, but you are almost sure it is true. When you access such a belief, STEP onto the paper labeled, 'Uncertainty leaning toward believing.' Feel what it feels like to feel not completely sure, but fairly sure."*

8. **Break, Then Set up Absolutely Certain:**
"Step off the papers to a mini-meta position (star between states), *and from an observer position, look at the space marked, "Absolutely Certain." What is something you believe STRONGLY. What is something you are willing to die for? What is something you believe absolutely? What are you certain about?"*

9. *"Now, return to the first position, Meta-Position A"*

B will now lead A through each of the nine locations, without using the star locations or "mini-meta-positions" indicated on the diagram. This is because the correct anchor has been established for each piece of paper.

Leading A onward…

1. *"Now, from this first Meta-Position A, just observe the papers with mild curiosity. Then step forward to the 'Limiting Belief About Self' paper."*

2. A states their specific "Limiting Belief About Self" while standing on the paper for, "Limiting Belief About Self." *"How has it felt to have and believe this idea? Say goodbye to this way of thinking about it as you 'carry this belief into the space of,' Uncertainty, leaning toward not true…"*

3. Invite the person both onto the paper, and into the state of, "Uncertainty, leaning toward not true…"

4. State, *"Now bring that uncertain belief to rest here in the "Museum of Old Beliefs." This is where you can park this belief, along with other things you used to believe, like… (list things like Santa Claus, The Tooth Fairy…) And when you are ready, step off into the Meta-Position B space, and just observe."*

5. Have the person take a moment in the Meta-Position B space, and assure they are disassociated and in observer mode..

6. B leads A into believing in the new belief with, *"Now step into this new belief, this well-formed belief you want in your life. Speak it to me. Say it. Tell me about how it feels at this point to believe this at whatever level you currently believe it.*

7. *"Now carry this belief into the, "Uncertain but leaning toward true" space. Make it look and sound and feel like something else probably true, but not so much as to be certain yet. Check inside and see if any parts object to this shift."*

8. *"Now carry this leaning toward true into the space of Absolute Certainty. Feel what it feels like to solidly believe and feel the strength of this as conviction."*

9. *"And now, just to be certain, carry this new, solid belief across the path,* (dashed arrow or step 9.) in the diagram) *into the same location where you first thought about the belief you have changed* (This would be space #2, the location where they used to "have" their limiting belief) *Check to make certain the change is good for all parts of you and your life."*

10. Future-pace and ecology check any proposed changes. *"From this space, think of a time in the future where this new belief will influence your behavior. Check to make sure you like the new changes."*

This method of changing beliefs appears to have limited use, but this is incorrect. It is not just for therapists and coaches working with someone who consciously wants to change a limiting belief. You can learn how to do the entire sequence with language alone.

This entire belief change process is a sequence of states. You can anchor states in a huge variety of ways – by touch, by gesture, by voice shifting, by leaning onto a different foot, by making a specific facial expression. I often work on changing people's beliefs while I am sitting in a restaurant and use items on the table as anchors for the various positions. I ask a person about one of the states involved in changing beliefs, and I pick up a sugar packet, holding it while I talk about the state associated with that "location." Then, when I want to sequence the states, picking up a sugar packet is unconsciously anchored to one of the states. So I change their beliefs by fiddling with the salt shaker, then the pepper shaker, then picking up a sugar packet. And suddenly, they feel like they are a worthwhile person.

Or, you can change beliefs in yourself extremely quickly using this technique if you set up anchors on the backs of your hands/knuckles for each of the states involved. Make your index finger knuckle the "Meta" position. Anchor the other knuckles (middle, ring and pinkie finger knuckles) to each of the states in the sequence shown in changing beliefs. You make one hand the, "Drop this belief off in the museum of things I used to believe" side, and the other the, "Take this idea and make it into a solid belief and try it on" side.

If you enjoy the parts and reframing model from HABTsm training (taught in the class called, "Resolving Conflicts – Inside and Out"), you can "Create a Part" and "teach" this process to the part. Then have it seek out limiting beliefs while you sleep, and take you through this process while you sleep. With permission, you could also help someone else build such a part in themselves.

The entire field of NLP is enhanced when people try to push a model to the Nth degree and see what it can do. Use your imagination to find ways you can influence another person's imagination in ways that offer them more of what they want in life.

Changing Beliefs Using Sub-Modalities

Of all the different models in NLP, I believe that the submodalities model has the broadest applications. You will easily find a million different ways to use this model, once you begin to master the subtle nuances of how to work with it. There is a very "overt" side to working with submodalities that is taught in almost any advanced NLP training. You can learn techniques for working with different problems, and for maximizing motivation and commitment. There are also a huge number of very subtle aspects to submodalities work that I was taught in Design Human Engineering™ training.

What is a Submodality - If we start with the visual **mode**, we are referring to pictures or images people make or have stored in their mind. These images have a location – which we will explore in just a moment. Thus location is a **sub-modality** of the visual mode. There are dozens of other potentially significant visual submodalities such as size of the image, brightness, its distance from you, color versus black-and-white and others. The auditory mode has submodalities that include volume, location, timbre and others. Changing submodalities is a powerful model for changing a person's experience of the world.

Overview

I remember watching videos of Richard Bandler training or working with clients over and over again, hoping to learn more of the layers he had encoded into these (by now very old) examples. After completing my second (of three times through) DHE™ training, I got to see another old video of Richard Bandler working with a client. I nearly fainted! There they were – all the things I had taught in DHE™ - right in front of my face. They were just too subtle to catch without that specific training.

One of the things I realized before anyone told me was that you could anchor a "set of submodalities" just as easily as you could a state. I began to wonder about the relationship between states and submodalities. This is not my favorite change arena, but it has an ocean of discovery waiting inside it, if anyone would like to swim in it!

In his "Neurosonics" tapes set and other training products, as well as many of his workshops, Richard Bandler works with the "location" of beliefs. Location is an extremely important submodality. In all sensory modalities! A slight twinge of cramping or pain located in our heads might lead us to seek aspirin, while the same twinge of cramping or pain located in our rectum might lead us to go to a doctor quickly. Fortunately, most of us can tell the difference between a pain in the… oh, you get the idea! Location of a sensory experience is important in almost all submodality work.

There is an easy way to experience this yourself. One of the famous "discovery games" you can play with submodalities is to think of someone you like, or like being around. Imagine or form a picture of that specific individual. Think of them, and notice "where in space" is the picture located? Literally point to it with your finger. Enjoy that image, and then let that image dissolve. Now imagine someone you dislike, or someone you dislike being around. Imagine or form a picture of that specific individual. Think of that individual, and notice "where in space" is the picture located? Again, point to that image with your finger. For most people, the images are on opposite sides. One group will be "off to the left," and one group will be "off to the right." The difference in location is a difference in **the location submodality of the visual mode.**

> **IMPORTANT NOTE**: Most often when I do this in a training, therapists ask, "So what does it **mean** that they have those pictures on the right side instead of their left?" There is no room for such "meaning" in the submodalities model. It doesn't "mean" anything. It is simply an observation. Most therapists are not satisfied with this, and they invent their own meanings anyway – which fits their model. These assumptions are inaccurate, and such assumptions will quickly make your submodalities work ineffective. They simply ARE on one side, and use that information to make your intervention effective. Stop making up explanations for things that do not need explanation! I have literally thrown therapists out of training programs when they start this, "I know better than you that there is a 'why' hiding here, and I'm going to

figure it out/make it up." They then begin "hiding" during the exercises – and I find them trying to mix their therapy model with a completely incompatible model.

Much of the belief change work done within the submodalities model is based on the same type of differences. First, you think of something you strongly believe, or are VERY certain about. It can be something extremely simple like, "The sun will come up tomorrow." Or it can be a very core religious value, or something you are absolutely sure of about yourself. Think of this belief, and form an image of that belief. It can be whatever comes to mind, or you can form a sort of "icon" for that belief. Again, notice the location of this image – the location for things you think are "definitely true." Then, let the image dissolve. Now, think of a belief you are not-so-sure about. It could be something you have considered but haven't decided about. It could be something not very important, or something you are still considering. If none of those "internal questions" bring up images, it can also be something you are somewhat sure is not true. Notice the location for things you think are either not true, or you are not so sure about. Again, the location for images of things you are sure are true, and the location for images of things you are not sure about are most likely two different locations. If they are the exact same location (which is possible but not likely), then some other "quality" of the image is your "driver" for believing it – such as clarity of the image, color vs. black and white, or some other specific quality of images in that location. But most often, location works just fine to create significant belief changes.

I have done belief changes with people and they thought I was just sort of "playing" with them or "joking around," and suddenly, they are amazed to find that they actually have a significant change in their thinking! Most often I have used what I call, "Slingshot beliefs." I have the person imagine a large rubber band wrapping around both of their ears (and I go through the gestures and motions of this!) and then I pull the rubber band out, "load" a belief into it and go "WHACK" and have the new belief go flying into their mind. Often people think it is just a "game" or a diversion. That is always nice, because it allows me to do all of the preliminary anchoring sequences, hypnotic language patterns, movement and submodality shifting without them paying any attention to it – because they assume I am just "playing around." I like to have fun, and I like for my client's to have fun. I also insist that they get the changes they wanted. I like to do all of those things at once.

Another way I do this is to play, "Belief Primordial Soup," where a sort of "no-zone" is established in a person's mind, and they just "allow" beliefs to form out of this "idea soup." This is a great way to get ecological target beliefs, because if they don't like the belief that rises up out of the soup, they can always dissolve it by pushing it back in, and inviting some other ideas to "rise up." This works very well with limiting metaphors as well, and was taught to me in the context of working with metaphors by Mr. Charles Faulkner, who has done amazing research and made major discoveries in the field of metaphors.

Another way to change or shift beliefs is to realize that some beliefs we believe "a lot," and some beliefs we believe "a little." You can imagine a lever or "volume knob" for the "amount" that you believe something, and adjust it accordingly. You practice and establish the control by imagining something you strongly believe, and imagining the knob or lever turned all the way up. You then imagine something that you only believe a little, and imagine the knob turned way down. You have to practice with several different beliefs at different levels to "calibrate the machine" and establish the connection for the anchoring. You can then think of beliefs that are limiting you, and "turn down your belief" in those ideas. Simultaneously, you can think of good quality "target beliefs," and simply turn the knob all the way up. This begins to scratch the surface of some techniques I learned from owning my own synthesizer, and that began to get REALLY expanded in Design Human Engineering™ training! This method also blurs the distinction between changing beliefs by changing states and changing beliefs by changing submodalities – because you can notice they will both shift together when you turn the knob.

Changing Beliefs Using Strategies

The only person I have seen teach strategies well and clearly is Charles Faulkner. Strategies are usually the least preferred and least understood portion of NLP training, and yet all of NLP can be seen as coming from strategies. Strangely enough, I have not seen any NLP organization teach the strategies model in over 20 years. Training on the strategies model is still available from Expanding Enterprises, Inc. via a class called, "Duplicating Competence."

Overview

In working with beliefs, we come into the notion of what are called, "Convincer strategies." Early in the world of cognitive studies, people began to study the process of becoming convinced of something. A lot of material has been written about how to convince people of things. Entire religions are based on the ability to convince others of the "rightness" of certain beliefs. Fortunately or unfortunately, most religious groups just did things like holding a sword to your throat and asking you what you believed, rather than actually learn and practice "running convincer strategies."

Earlier in this book, we talked about how people must have an event happen in the world in order to claim that there is evidence for them to believe that something is true. This is especially true in rule-based belief systems. We also stated that this evidence must be sensory based – that it must be something the person sees with their eyes, hears with their ears, or feels in their body. It may also be something they smell or taste, but that is much less likely. We also mentioned that often what is considered evidence for something is not always the best evidence to use. For example, many spouses have as evidence that their spouse loves them because they abuse them. Often therapists attempt to change the evidence, without an understanding the larger whole of how belief structures work and fit together. That rarely ever works.

Early in the days of NLP, it was discovered that convincer strategies – the way in the strategies model that we decide things are facts in the world – are "two-level strategies." They include a program and a sub-routine. A sub-routine is a computer program that "runs in the background" of another program, and often uses data or output from the first program in its routine. We have already presented the first "routine" of convincer strategies in our model of belief diagramming. That is, a person needs sensory-based evidence to become convinced that some quality or event exists in the world. However, just seeing something happen once is often not enough to truly convince them that this is "certainly the case." It often takes a bit more to totally convince someone of the facts of something. This is especially true for process-based belief systems.

The "bit more" or next level of evidence is the sub-routine of convincer strategies, and it involves one of four different convincer subroutines:

1.) Number of times the evidence was experienced
2.) Period of time over which the evidence was experienced
3.) One existing example – automatically convinced
4.) Never fully convinced

The most common or frequent convincer subroutine is the first one, number of times. And the most common number of times needed to become convinced of something is three. That is why three is considered "The Magic Number" when you are delivering language patterns, when you are "yupping" your client, or when you are attempting to convince people. You want to always "package" your ideas in groups of three. I have done it over and over and over again in this book. This paragraph itself contains two examples of this process.

What this "number of times" means is, how many times must that particular sensory evidence appear in your world before you will give it the status of really existing independent of your searching for it.

You ask for evidence by asking, "How do you know that _____ exists?" This can be nearly anything, so let me provide several examples – maybe even three of them.

You may ask someone, "How do you know that one of your co-workers is a good employee?" They may reply, "I **see** that they do good paperwork." Thus you know that the evidence is visual evidence – seeing good paperwork the person has done. You then want to inquire about the convincer subroutine. So you could ask, "And how many times would you have to see them do good paperwork before you would be convinced that they were a good employee?" This is a very targeted question that most people actually have not thought about, and so they often shrug and reply, "I don't know." You want to "push" for an answer, so you can offer a menu – "Once? Five times? Ten times?" You will discover that most people will say, "Two or three I guess." You then know that their convincer strategy **FOR THIS CONTEXT** is:

Level 1 = Visual Evidence (See good paperwork)
Level 2 = Number of Times (Two or three times. If they say "two or three," go with three.)

This is by far the most common convincer strategy. I have become convinced of this.

When I worked at a state mental health facility, I got transferred to a new ward to work with a new team of people. Contrary to the glorious reputation that state employees enjoy in the general public, there were a small number who did actually live up to the title of "goldbrickers." They worked hard to avoid doing any actual work by constantly snapping, "That's not my job!" They spent their days socializing in their office, and they relied upon political maneuvers to keep their jobs rather than doing any actual work. As a result of their efforts, the other employees had to work twice as hard to cover for them, including often doing their paperwork for them so that they could get their own paperwork done. Where I worked, all of the offices were in a long hallway. I remember quietly walking down the hallway on many occasions, just to see what the other employees were doing. I realized that what I was doing was hoping to see them leaning over their desks, writing on papers. If I saw a particular individual doing that on three of my walks down the hall, I became convinced they were a "good co-worker." Three of my co-workers "earned" the status of "good co-worker" in my first three days on the new unit. Another one NEVER got to be a "good co-worker" in my mind, because every single time I walked down the hallway, she was "entertaining another guest" in her office – and they were definitely NOT patients she was counseling!

At one point, this woman confronted me about my "walks down the hall." I told her with a smile that I was, "…checking up on everybody, to see if they were a good co-worker, working like little bees in their office." She rolled her eyes at me and said, "Honey, THAT'S not how you know a good co-worker." I knew she was about to tell me her convincer strategy, so I said with curiosity, "Well, how can I tell?" She replied, "You gotta keep your ears open. A bad co-worker is somebody who 'bad-mouths' you behind your back." I looked at her puzzled and said, "Well, everybody says not-so-nice things sometimes. How many times would somebody have to 'bad-mouth' me before I decide they are a bad co-worker?" She replied, "No no no. You listen for a while. If they keep bad-mouthing you for a month, you can bet they will keep doing it."

In this statement, she revealed all the routines of her convincer strategy for bad co-worker:

Level 1 = Auditory evidence (**Hearing** them "bad-mouth" you – i.e. speaking negatively about you)
Level 2 = Period of time ("If they keep bad-mouthing you for **a month**…")
And just as an aside, this woman bad-mouthed everybody behind their backs constantly, and also met all of my criteria for "goldbricker" on a constant basis.

When I worked as a caseworker at that hospital, I wrote treatment plans, and I turned them in to my boss. My boss would review them, and if he approved of them, he would send them off to be put into the patient's treatment record. I had the same boss for many years, and he reviewed every single treatment plan carefully. When I learned about convincer strategies, I went to him and asked him how he knew if a treatment plan was a "good treatment plan." He smiled and said, "I read them carefully, and if they have 'flow' and clarity and make sense, I approve them." I then asked him, "How many times does a caseworker have to write a good treatment plan before you believe they just write good treatment plans?" He looked at me puzzled, then smiled and said, "I read EVERY treatment plan. Just because the last two or even the last 100 were good, I still read them carefully. Just because somebody DID write a good treatment plan doesn't mean the next one will be equally as good."

In these statements, he revealed all of the routines of his convincer strategy:

Level 1 = Visual or auditory evidence = ("I read them carefully.")
    Note: Some people claim that reading is visual. They have to SEE it on the page. However, words on a page do not have any meaning at all unless you read them – which, for most people, means speak them inside of their head. So most often, "reading" indicates AUDITORY evidence. – they have to hear the words spoken inside their head. For him, it was auditory. I also discovered that part of his flow criteria (notice the abstract evidence) had to do with the sentences having good rhythm!
Level 2 = Never fully convinced.

What I found fascinating was that once I knew that his convincer strategy in this context included never being fully convinced, I simply accepted that he would read, edit and return for corrections my treatment plans for the rest of my career. Some employees were HORRIBLY insulted by his editing and corrections, and felt he was picking on them. I interpreted it as him caring enough about our work and about the treatment plans that he checked on things.

In contrast, when I got transferred to another unit to work with a different supervisor, he never checked my work or my treatment plans. Instead, when I brought them to him, he would glance at them, hand them back to me and say, "Looks great." So, of course, I asked him, "How do you know that a treatment plan is a good treatment plan?" He shrugged and said, "I know you, and I know your treatment plans. I read the first one you did very carefully and I realized you knew how to write them well, and I didn't need to keep looking over your shoulder or telling you how to write them."

In this statement, he gave me all of the routines of his convincer strategy:

Level 1 = Auditory ("I **read** the first one you did very carefully…)
Level 2 = One existing example or automatically convinced ("I read **the first one**…)

A person may use different convincer strategies in different contexts. For example, ask a parent, "How do you know your kid is a good kid?" In this context, you actually never want them to be fully convinced, so that they will keep checking on an ongoing basis. How many times has a parent been confronted about their kid doing drugs or getting into trouble at school, and they reply, "Not MY child!!" What they are actually saying is, "I have already RUN my convincer strategy that my child is a good child, and no counter-evidence is allowed! After all, I have three examples from his youth!"

I once taught a training that included convincer strategies where four women from the same agency sat up front near me. One of them was the supervisor of the other three. I made it very, very clear to the people involved that I was **not** asking the supervisor how she knew any of the people under her supervision were good employees, but I wanted to know how she knew her co-workers who did the same job she did were good employees. She answered, "I see the statistical reports on their work every week." (Level 1 = Visual evidence – seeing reports. She added they were graphs.) I then asked, "Ok, and how many times do you have to see those reports looking a certain way before you are convinced they are a good employee?" She replied, "Well, actually, I have to see those reports looking good for about a month and a half before I am convinced they do their job well." (Level 2 = Period of time – 1.5 months.) Before I could even outline her strategy on the board, one of the employees under her looked over at her infuriated and cried out, "A month and a half!! For crying out loud, woman! You just need to see them things two or three times and that should tell you right there that they know their job!" (Level 1 = Visual evidence; Level 2 = Number of times.) As I tried to make explicit the difference in their strategies, a third woman added quite angrily, "I think you are both nuts! If you want to find out if someone is a good employee, you go talk to their co-workers. If they tell you they are a good worker, you're done! All them reports don't mean nothing!" (Level 1 = Auditory evidence; Level 2 = One existing example.) And, not to be left out, the fourth woman nodded at the third and said, "That's right. You should ask their co-workers to find out if they are any good. And keep asking them, 'cause they might slip up once in a while, so you just keep checking in." (Level 1 = Auditory evidence; Level 2 = Never fully convinced.) I spent a great deal of time explaining how everyone feels THEIR convincer strategy is the RIGHT one, and that people will definitely argue and fight about "which" convincer strategy is the correct one. While the rest of the class learned an extremely quick lesson in convincer strategy differences, the four women who had gotten into this argument completely "missed" what they were arguing about, and never did fully get the information about convincer strategies. The other people in the class will probably never forget convincer strategies and how powerfully they work!

One More Distinction about Evidence and Convincing

I have a friend who falls in love constantly, immediately and deeply - with disastrous results. When I asked him how he knows if a woman loves him, he replied, "When I feel a stirring in my heart when I'm in her presence." When I asked him how many times he has to feel this stirring in his heart, he replied, "Just once." Thus we know his strategy is:

Level 1 = Kinesthetic evidence ("When I feel a stirring in my heart…")
Level 2 = One existing example ("Just once.")

His evidence brings up another common difficulty in convincer strategies and evidence – his evidence for this **external** event is entirely **internal** evidence! He does not even utilize how her face looks when she looks at him, the voice tone she uses when she speaks to him – or any other external event. He utilizes completely **internal evidence**. People who utilize completely internal evidence are extremely easy to influence by shifting their states.

You need to practice listening for and eliciting convincer strategies from people. As you learn to hear and "catch" a person's convincer strategy, you learn another level of packaging any belief change work you want to do with a person. This strategy helps you present your information in a way that the person is more likely to believe it – which is incredibly valuable when you are trying to change beliefs. Often people assume you are asking about their convincer strategies because you intend to "borrow" their convincer strategy. They may become defensive or guarded if you present your question is if you are challenging their strategy. Be curious. People are amazing in their variety and uniqueness, as well as their similarities and patterns. As you begin to notice what it takes for people to become convinced of different ideas, work to help convince them that:

1.) They are deeply loved and appreciated – (by someone other than you, or they will refuse to ever go away!)
2.) They are worthwhile
3.) They can succeed
4.) They are uniquely wonderful

THESE are the kind of beliefs I recommend you practice "installing" into people as we move on to the most powerful tool for shifting beliefs – language!

Section 4: Changing Beliefs with Language and NLP Models

Weakening Beliefs with NLP Models

Let's start with ways to utilize NLP models and language to weaken beliefs that the client has identified that they want to change.

We will first teach you statements to weaken ("Sleight-of-Mouth") a belief, and then patterns to strengthen (Presuppositions) beliefs with language. We do this because you often want to weaken a current belief, then introduce and presuppose a more ecological belief when you are doing belief change, rather than trying to just "overpower" the old belief. There are several additional ways to weaken or strengthen beliefs that do not involve language.

Weakening Beliefs with States

When using this technique, begin by asking the person about things they don't believe very strongly, or ideas they used to believe and later found out were not true. Establish a discreet non-verbal behavior (an anchor) such as a look or gesture, and keep demonstrating the exact same behavior/anchor each time they discuss feeling uncertain, feeling like they no longer believe it, or feeling doubtful. The non-verbal behavior will become "paired" with the state of "not believing." Then, ask them about the belief they want to change, and "fire the anchor" or demonstrate the same behavior. You will be leading them into a state of non-believing while they talk about the belief. This can be done incredibly obviously, and most people will not consciously notice what you are doing. This is an extremely powerful influence technique that many therapists are already constantly using, but are not aware they are doing it to their clients.

Weakening Beliefs with Submodalities

Ask them about something they used to believe, something they feel uncertain about, or something about which they feel doubtful. Look for gestures, glances or other non-verbal submodality cues that indicate "where" in the space around them do they "store" things they don't really believe. Then ask them about the belief they want to change, notice the cues for its current location, and gently gesture as if you were "moving" the idea to the location of non-believing. If you do this while you are using language patterns, it is an incredibly powerful combination.

Use both of these methods listed above as you utilize the language patterns shown in the remainder of this section to both weaken and then strengthen beliefs.

Changing Beliefs with Language

One of the fastest and easiest ways to influence beliefs is to utilize language skills that are specifically designed to influence others. In fact, the remainder of this book will focus on using language patterns in strategic ways to help you influence beliefs.

There are two main categories of belief shifting language patterns. The first is generally aimed at helping to weaken or "challenge" limiting beliefs. The second set of language patterns is generally aimed at helping to "install" or "strengthen" beliefs.

Part 1: Weakening Beliefs – "Sleight-of-Mouth"

Advanced NLP training includes a section called, "Sleight-of-Mouth." (Hereafter called SOM). There is a "list" of SOM patterns, and they are generally taught as a list. Very little information is available about which SOM pattern to use with which type of person or in which type of setting. Often, people just practice by trying different ones with different people until something seems to work. Most often people learning SOM tend to learn and practice only the forms that work on THEM. They tend to "discard" the other forms, and often don't even practice them.

From the very beginning, I became fascinated with why some patterns worked well with some people, and other patterns worked well with other people. Nobody could tell me what the "difference that made a difference" was in this context. It took me four years of studying, experimenting, working and playing to finally discover some patterns, and one of the reasons for writing this book was to make my observed patterns explicit.

One of the ways I practiced SOM patterns was by taking a single pattern, and using it over and over again all day long. The next day, I would take a different SOM pattern and use only that pattern all day long. This helped prevent my only using the patterns that worked for myself, and helped me to realize the different patterns that work with different types of people. It is also why I developed the NLP practice cards I sell that include a set of SOM cards, and a set of Presuppositional Forms cards. These cards include examples of a programmed learning via color and font structuring that I developed as part of my thesis in Education in their design as well, to help you learn the categories and notice some new distinctions.

Part 2: Strengthening Beliefs – Presuppositions

Presuppositions are the most powerful form of communication with the other-than-conscious mind. By learning to "stack" presuppositions together, you can learn to make your communication produce multiple impacts with a single communication. We will help the client to build the new belief by speaking "As if" the new belief were already true.

Part 1:
Using Sleight-of-Mouth

The Four Categories of SOM Patterns

I have often seen Sleight-of-Mouth (SOM) patterns taught just as a list of sentences. However, it is very difficult to just learn a list – and I have discovered some very interesting distinctions within the SOM patterns. Also, having experimented for years, I have found that certain SOM patterns work better with certain types of people.

First, let's look at the four different types or categories of SOM patterns

1. *Time – Here, time has two meanings. It may mean "time" as in past, present and future or a long duration, or it may mean "instance" – as in the first "time" something has happened. In time patterns, time or duration of a belief is questioned. Or, the meaning assigned to a particular instance of something is presupposed, or challenged.*

2. **Existence -** In these patterns, the existence of something is presumed, or the meaning of the evidence is questioned or re-defined. Context and content reframing are part of these forms.

3. **Quality – These patterns shift beliefs by directing attention to how the belief fits into other parts or pieces of the person's belief structure. They may change scope, or change criteria, or shift frames.**

4. **Meaning** – These patterns are SOM patterns that influence the person to think that their belief about the world is just an idea, not a factual understanding. They also invite the listener to re-examine the belief and possibly form different ideas from the same evidence.

Now let's examine the different SOM patterns.

Sleight-of-Mouth Patterns: Layout Example

The SOM patterns will all be presented with the following format:

Title of the SOM Form:
(A comment about the SOM form)
[If needed, what the person stated as their belief may be given]

"Saying what you find here would be an example of 'using' this SOM pattern."

- A note about how this SOM pattern creates influence/change in beliefs

When to use this pattern: Suggestions for how to know when and with whom you should utilize this particular SOM pattern.

Formatted Example of a Specific SOM Pattern: "Reality Strategy"

Reality Strategy:
(Asking for their evidence, or about how they constructed that belief.)

"What makes you say that?"
"How do you know that's true?"
"Where'd you get that idea from?" (sic)
"Who told you that?"

- This pattern invites the listener to examine the connection between the frame and the evidence, and questions the validity of the conclusion or connection.

When to use this pattern: Incongruence when stating the belief, or beliefs that seem outdated or naive.

Time SOM Patterns

Three of the SOM patterns are very obviously related to time, and two are more related to "instancing."

Time SOM Patterns

<u>Time:</u>
"How long have you thought of this in this way?"
"For how long have you believed Martians were lazy?"
"So at this point in time, you think...(re-state belief.)

- This pattern invites the listener to place a sort of "bookmark" on their timeline, and the believing of the idea becomes associated with the point in time. This then allows them to imagine a time when they no longer believe this to be a "fact" any longer.

When to use this pattern: Between-time sorting - people who do a lot of comparisons, comparing this instance with that instance, this event with that event, etc. In terms of NLP Meta-Programs, this pattern works best with people who use the two-step comparisons like Same-Difference or Difference-Same

<u>Consequences:</u>
(Exploring the consequences of them continuing to believe the idea.)
"If you continue to believe this, your brain cells will melt together and rot."
"You keep thinking like that and it will never work out."
"Thinking like that will help you stay on track"
"Ideas like that must make you very unpopular with the Martians."

- This pattern leads the listener to attach a negative (or positive) state to the maintaining of this belief. The state then gets generalized or simply paired with the belief, which biases the person toward either keeping or changing the belief.

When to use this pattern: In-time sorting – people who have a timeline that goes "front-to-back," and often get "lost" inside of their experiences. It also works better for people with more C-E belief structures.

Prior Cause:
(Attributing the believing of something to an earlier "excuse," cause, or reason.)
"You only believe that because you had a rough childhood."
"You only believe that because your mother toilet trained you at gunpoint."
"I can understand how you would think that way, given what you've told me about your past."
"I know all the past Martians you have met have been lazy, but times are changing."

- This pattern leads the listener to shift their attention away from whether the belief stands on its own as a fact, and attributes the believing of it to some other cause. This allows them an opportunity to experiment with not believing it for a moment, or makes them question the state of "true" being associated with this particular belief.

When to use this pattern: Through-time sorting; people who have a "left-to-right" timeline, and who disassociate easily to compare. Between-time people stay associated when they compare and "try on" the two states. Through-time people disassociate and compare in a more abstract fashion. In terms of Meta-Programs, this form works best on difference sorters.

Model of the World 1:
(The "Only YOU believe this" frame)
"So for YOU..."
"So the way you DESCRIBE/VIEW/SEE/SUPPOSE this situation..."

- This pattern leads the listener to re-evaluate the accuracy of their belief by framing it as something only THEY think. You could just say, "Well I don't believe that, and neither do most experts." But this particular frame is much less "challenging," and simply invites them to experience the belief as less like a fact, and more like an idea.

When to use this pattern: Externally referenced individuals

Counter-Example:
(Keeping the same frame, but the generalization doesn't "hold up" for another example or person.)

[Stated belief: "You are late and that means you don't care about me."]
"Well, your elderly grandfather is often late, but nobody ever questions HIS caring."

[Stated belief: "You don't tell me you love me, so I don't believe you do."]
"The kids don't tell you they love you, but do you question their love?"

[Stated belief: "You charge money for this, so it doesn't come from your heart."]
"You get paid when you show up for work. Does that mean your heart isn't in your work?"

[Stated belief: "All Martians are lazy."]
"The Martian ambassador not only works hard at his job, he's on four committees."

- This pattern reduces the "generalizability" of their belief by indicating that the same evidence does NOT prove the belief in other situations. The unspoken conclusion is that it should not prove the belief in THIS situation either.

When to use this pattern: People who strongly value congruence and fairness

Existence SOM Patterns

These patterns challenge the evidence, or the "rule" that has been generalized from the particular piece of evidence. They work best on "rule-based" belief systems.

Existence SOM Patterns

Challenge:
(Good old-fashioned disagreeing! Or, claiming that their evidence proves nothing.)
      "That's not true."
      "You don't really believe that, do you?"

- This pattern leads the listener to evaluate their level of "certainty" about the belief, and if they respect you as an authority, they may attempt to change or delete the belief. It should be used carefully, because sometimes people have beliefs that they KNOW are actually not true – but they believe them anyway.

When to use this pattern: They deliver the belief statement incongruently, or they respect you as an authority.

Reality Strategy:
(Asking for their evidence, or about how they constructed that belief.)

      "What makes you say that?"
      "How do you know that's true?"
      "Where'd you get that idea from?" (sic)
      "Who told you that?"

- This pattern invites the listener to examine the connection between the frame and the evidence, and questions the validity of the conclusion or connection.

When to use this pattern: Incongruence when stating the belief, or beliefs that seem outdated or naive.

Redefine:
(Claiming that the same evidence ACTUALLY proves something else.) (Content reframing)

[Stated belief: "Your arriving late means you don't care."]
"I'm late because I take great care to get here safely and well prepared so I can really enjoy being with you."

[Stated belief: "Laughing means you're not taking this seriously."]
"My laughing means I'm relaxed and willing to look at this from many different perspectives."

[Stated belief: "Martians are lazy."]
"It's not that they're lazy, they just consider things carefully and think a long time before they make a decision."

- This pattern gets them to change the title of the frame – that the evidence really proves something other than what they called it.

When to use this pattern: Any time!

Analogy/Metaphor:

(Mentioning a situation in which the same evidence might mean something different. Often a metaphoric counter-example from another context.) (Context reframing)

[Stated belief: "You not coming to my party means you aren't my friend."
   "A party is like a big, busy henhouse – where no one particular hen matters much at all."
   "Well, people came to your party who were not your friends."
   "I've made lots of time for you when you weren't having any party."
   "Being with you in a crowd just dilutes any special moment we could have."

[Stated belief: "All Martians are lazy."]
   "Martians are like turtles. They don't hurry, but they get there."

- Think of another context in the world where this is not a good belief, or a different context where this is not the case.

When to use this pattern: Any time!

Switch Referential Index:

(A counter-example in another person or context.) (Context reframing)
(Think of another person in their world for whom this statement is not true, or a different context where this same evidence clearly proves something different.)

[Stated belief: "You not coming to my party means you aren't my friend."]
   "Well, your parents didn't come to your party, and you consider that a good thing!"
   "I hate parties, and I thought as my friend you would understand that."
   "I never go to anybody's parties. Ever."

[Stated belief: "All Martians are lazy."]
   "So why did they travel 2 million miles to get here?"

When to use this pattern: Any time!

Chunk Size:

(Focusing on the smallness of their evidence, or exaggerating the vastness of their generalization.)

[Stated belief: "Your being late means you don't care about me."]

"So being 13 minutes late for our meeting means I don't care about you at all?"

[Stated belief: "You not coming to my party means you aren't my friend."]

"So every single other friend you have in the world was at your party?"

"So helping you shop to prepare for the party doesn't count?"

[Stated belief: "You not spending half your waking hours with the kids means you are not a good father."]

"So spending 7.5 instead of 8.0 hours per day with them means I'm not a good father?"

[Stated belief: "All Martians are lazy."]

So every single one of them is completely lazy?"

When to use this pattern: Cause-effect system structure or strongly "rule-bound" individuals

Quality SOM Patterns

These patterns use "other beliefs" to leverage a change in beliefs. They are very useful in state-based beliefs, because they invoke other states (by invoking other beliefs) than the ones usually accessed by the belief.

Quality SOM Patterns

<u>**Hierarchy of Criteria:**</u>

(Jumping to a more highly valued criteria, and placing it "at odds" with the current belief. Requires that you know something about the person's values, and in particular about very important beliefs/values in their belief system.)

[Stated belief: "Your being late means you don't care about me."]
"Please give me a fair chance to show you I care."
(Assuming the person values "fairness.")

[Stated belief: "You not coming to my party means you aren't my friend."]
"I was busy taking care of my sick grandmother."
(Assuming the person values "taking care of others or ill people.")

[Stated belief: "All Martians are lazy."]
"Do you think it's efficient to think of all of them that way?"

When to use this pattern: When you are certain you know some of their highly valued criteria

Meta-Frame:
(Jumping to a much higher or larger frame in which the current evidence and criteria are irrelevant.)

    [Stated belief: "Your being late means you don't care about me."]

        "So you want to know you are cared about in a good relationship."

            (Changes frame from, "You are late here and now" to "Our relationship."

        "I enjoy spending time with you, and I also don't like when something reduces that time."

            (Changes frame from, "I am late carelessly" to "Our time together.")

    [Stated belief: "You not coming to my party means you aren't my friend."]

        "But there are a lot of other ways you know I am your friend."

            (Changes frame to other social "clues" of friendship.)

        "I know your social life is very important to you."

            (Changes frame from "this party" to "your social life.")

    [Stated belief: "All Martians are lazy."]

        "So having everybody working hard is that important to you?"

When to use this pattern: When you know something about their different frames and domains

Frame Size:
(Changing the focus to a much larger and more inclusive frame, or restricting to a very small frame.)

[Stated belief: "Your being late means you don't care about me."]
"Does everyone in your world have to live up to every single one of your expectations all the time?"
(Changes frame from "You're late tonight" to "Expectations of friends in my world.")
"Sometimes being 13 minutes late just means parking was really bad."
(Changes the frame size from "late" to "Only 13 minutes late.")

[Stated belief: "All Martians are lazy."]
"So every other species in the galaxy is lazy compared to us?"

When to use this pattern: Very rule-bound individuals and expectations

---

Intent:
(Attributing the belief to a larger belief system, or the holding of that belief to some positive intention.)
[Stated belief: "Your being late means you don't care about me."]
"You only believe that because you want to be fair to people."
"You only believe that because you are so careful about being prompt yourself."
"You only believe that to keep yourself driven and motivated."

[Stated belief: "All Martians are lazy."]
"You only believe that because you are so hard-working and efficient."

When to use this pattern: Any time!

Apply to (the belief it) Self:

(Apply the value or criteria word mentioned IN the belief TO the belief, or, to not having the belief itself.)

> [Stated belief: "I think people are stupid."
> **"That's a stupid belief."**
>
> [Stated belief: "Those people are bad."]
> **"That just bad thinking."**
>
> [Stated belief: "I love you."]
> **"I love you too, and I love that you feel that way about me!"**
>
> [Stated belief: "All Martians are lazy."]
> **"You're just too lazy to get to know them well."**
>
> **When to use this pattern**: Use whenever a value word is mentioned in a belief.

Self/Other:

(Asking about how another person might experience or interpret this same situation differently.)

> **"What would your mother say about that?"**
> **"Would your son/aunt/landlord/spouse agree with that idea?"**
>
> **When to use this pattern**: Use when you know the "other" mentioned is well respected or considered by them to be an authority.

Meaning SOM Patterns

These patterns are designed to change the meaning of the belief by changing the frame quality. They work best on state-based and rule-based beliefs.

Meaning SOM Patterns

Model of the World 2:
(Framing their belief as "something they only THINK is true.")

> "So you THINK…"
> "So you've been thinking that…"

When to use this pattern: Useful with very internally referenced people. Leads them to examine the "amount" or "level" of how convinced they are.

Questioning Tonal Shift:
(Saying their belief back to them, but with a rising or questioning tonal inflection at the end of the backtrack/belief.)

When to use this pattern: Useful with very externally referenced people.

Reversing Presuppositions: (Developed by Dr. Connirae Andreas)
(Inviting them to explore how something could mean exactly the opposite of what they are suggesting it means.)

> "In what way could (X) actually mean or cause the opposite of what you are suggesting?"
> "How could feeling hatred toward your children really mean you love them?"
> > ["Well, I hate when they misbehave, because I want them to be happy and well-adjusted, and when I see them behave like that, I fear for their futures!"]

"In what way	could	(X) actually	cause	the opposite of what you are suggesting?"
	does		equal	
	can		mean	
	could			
	has			
	would			
	might			

When to use this pattern: When they are totally stuck in something meaning only one thing

---

Tonal Emphasis on Frame: (Developed by Larry Westenberg)

[Stated belief: "Your being late means you don't care about me."]
"So in the world of FRIENDS, timeliness is obviously pretty important to you."
"If we were just BUSINESS PARTNERS, would it mean the same thing?"

[Stated belief: "All Martians are lazy."]
"So every species in the entire GALAXY is lazy compared to you?"

When to use this pattern: When you suspect a limited frame for the belief.

Naming the Frame: (Developed by Larry Westenberg)

[Stated belief: "Your being late means you don't care about me."]
"Why are we having a discussion about my caring?"
"You want to talk about timeliness?"
"Is this going to be a discussion about our relationship?"

[Stated belief: "All Martians are lazy."]
"So you want to talk about laziness in the world."

When to use this pattern: Any time!

Now that you have seen the entire set of SOM patterns, you will need to practice them a great deal in order to make them natural tools in a conversation.

Go to www.expandingenterprises.com and order the two sets of practice cards – one for SOM, the other for Presuppositions. They are literally designed to be small enough to fit in your hand so people do not see them if you are using them to practice.

Most often, people discover two or three of these patterns that work well on themselves, and they begin to think those few are the most powerful language patterns. Each of these patterns appeals to different brains. Learn them all, and notice the shifts in non-verbal behavior when one of them works.

Part 2:
Presuppositions

Presuppositions – Opposite of SOM

Presuppositions are the opposite of Sleight-of-Mouth. SOM "weakens" beliefs with questions that produce specific cognitive shifts. Presuppositions "strengthen beliefs by speaking about the desired outcome in a way that strengthens it. Okay, yes – you can use presuppositions to weaken things too.

Presuppositions are the most powerful form of communication with the other-than-conscious mind. By learning to "stack" presuppositions together, you can learn to make your communication almost irresistible to the listener. By learning to utilize customer's values and criteria in your presuppositions, you can learn to overcome resistance and create the mental and social environment to attain your outcomes, both in yourself and with others.

You will need all the basic elements in place to make presuppositions work for you:

- Rapport
- A clear outcome, and the associated meta-outcome
- An ecological outcome implementation plan
- Some idea of the customer's major values/criteria
- The skills you will begin learning here

Remember that throughout our books and our training classes we have been emphasizing the importance of practice to master the skills. This is nowhere more important than in the development of using presuppositions. In fact, this portion of the training is a workbook, designed to go with a presentation and training package on using presuppositions. While the ideas are really very simple, the process of "generating" sentences that create presuppositions must be practiced over and over to be fully mastered.

Here – I'll just say it as plainly as I can: If you want to be a "Change Ninja," you want to spend tons of time practicing presuppositions and Sleight-of-Mouth. "These aren't the droids you're looking for!" is just the tip of the iceberg… (A Star Wars reference from the first movie, for those too young to remember.)

I attended a class on Advanced Language Patterns that listed out all of the presuppositions, and I got to keep the huge flipchart notes. (Thank you, Charles!) At that time, I worked at the state psychiatric hospital. My office had a 15-foot high ceiling. I put the presuppositional forms that were written on huge flipchart paper high up on the wall that was right behind where my clients sat for counseling. I told them it was things I needed to memorize and that they were my flashcards. That was TRUE! I kept them there for over two years. Only one patient ever read them – and he got what they were!

If you immerse yourself in **either** SOM or presuppositions, you will get the other one quickly and easily.

What Is a Presupposition?

Each and every sentence you speak contains many presuppositions. Let's examine a very simple sentence:

"Fred and Sally went to the store."

While it is a simple sentence, it contains many presuppositions:

- There exists someone named Fred.
- There exists someone named Sally, and
- There exists a store.

Fred, Sally and store are all nouns. The mere presence of the words Fred, Sally and store simply assumes or "presupposes" that all of these entities exist. Their existence is not discussed or proven as part of this communication. Their existence is simply presupposed by the fact that they are mentioned in the sentence.

However, there is even MORE presupposed in this simple sentence:

- Fred and Sally did something in the past.

We know this because the word "went" is a verb, and it is a verb in the PAST TENSE.

This sentence also contains another presupposition -

- Fred and Sally went somewhere.

Did you ASSUME that they went to the store together? Notice that this fact is NOT stated in the sentence. But did you simply make an image of them going to the store together? Assumptions are REALATED to presuppositions, but they are also different.

Examples of Presuppositions Exercise

In groups of four, take turns reading one of these sentences to members of your small group. (Do not appoint one person to read all of them. All parties should both speak and listen to sentences. Also, do not read ahead or read them as the other person speaks them. Let them be surprises spoken to you.) As you listen to one of these sentences being read to you, pay close attention to your own internal experience – to any images you make in your mind, any feelings or other experiences you have.

1. Are there other things that you have learned easily?

2. It is playful presupposition practice that helps you learn them well.

3. Haven't you noticed how easy it is to use presuppositions?

4. If you should happen to not learn presuppositions, I would be surprised.

5. I wonder if you're not learning them without even trying.

6. Just hearing presuppositions helps you to learn them well.

7. If you weren't learning presuppositions, you wouldn't be so curious.

8. You can use presuppositions repeatedly in work and in social conversation.

9. You can also learn presuppositional forms from a book or tape.

10. While you learn about presuppositions, remember to have fun with them.

11. You can continue learning about presuppositions forever.

12. You can learn new ways to use presuppositions.

13. Is this the first time you have decided to learn about presuppositions?

14. You could easily become a person who uses presuppositions constantly.

15. Isn't it odd how easily you can learn to use presuppositions?

16. Learning to use presuppositions will happen faster than you expect.

17. You can learn to use presuppositions as easily as you learned to speak.

18. Fortunately, you can learn to use presuppositions unconsciously.

19. What is easiest to learn is the use of presuppositional questions.

20. What difference does it make if you don't learn them all today?

21. Have you already learned presuppositions from these examples?

How do Presuppositions Work?

Language and the brain are very interesting partners. Language or speech is processed unconsciously. So unless your ears are plugged, you will automatically process any statements people make to you. For example, if I say to you:

"Blue wombats are coming."

Most people instantly make a picture in their mind of some animals coming toward them. But are there such things as blue wombats? There are blue herons, and blue foxes... Why not blue wombats? Check inside and see if you made some type of pictures in your mind of these animals?

Now if I say to you:

"Blue wombats are coming in Toyota Convertibles."

Hey - does Toyota even make a convertible? Doesn't matter! Didn't you already make an image of one in your mind? And are those wombats driving that truck, or in a cage in the back of the truck? And how many wombats are there in your image? A hundred? See, our brain processes the information, and THEN decides whether or not it is true. And notice how willing your brain is to "stretch" to allow things like Toyota Convertibles to exist. Let's go one more:

"Blue wombats from Mars are driving here in Toyota convertibles."

Notice how your brain may even make an image, but then there is a very strong, "No!" Have you ever had salespeople call and say something like, "And would you like us to deliver that on Tuesday or Wednesday?" or some other statement that made you feel like, "No! No way!" Didn't you feel angry and in some strange way violated? That person went too far, too fast with their presuppositions, and you "snapped" into "No way." **You want to avoid this "snap," this going too far, at all costs!** Remember how willing your brain was to stretch with the first two sentences? (Or maybe only the first sentence.) Keep things in the stretch mode! Keep things SMALL!

Now, we don't want to convince people about blue wombats, but we do want to convince them that:

1. With your assistance, they will make a satisfying change
2. They are very satisfied with your services/assistance
3. They will be delighted to tell their friends about you
4. They feel good in their future change
5. Anything else useful...

You need to first brainstorm a list of what you want a customer to think and feel. What would be helpful to have a customer believe/value in their work with you? And what do they already believe that you want to reinforce – like the ideas listed above.

Brainstorming:

Write down ideas for each of the following categories. You may come up with your own ideas, work with your group, or get ideas from other groups. After the larger group has discussed and shared their favorites, **pick three favorites** to write in the boxes on the next page. These will be called our "Target Presuppositions." (You may want to copy this page.)

Five useful states for customers/self:
"I want (my customers) to feel - excited, confident, interested…"

_____

_____

_____

_____

Five useful attitudes about a plan of action:
"This plan – will work, is a good time investment…"

_____

_____

_____

_____

Five impressive facts about a particular action plan:
"This plan - uses your skills, will get you a raise, keeps you employed…"

_____

_____

_____

_____

Target Presuppositions:

Write down your **three favorite** ideas to presuppose, and write them in the boxes on this page. These will be called our "Target Presuppositions." (You may want to copy this page)

Three states:
"…excited, confident, interested…"

_____

_____

_____

Three attitudes:
"…confident, cooperative, appreciated…"

_____

_____

_____

Three facts:
"…gets you a raise, keeps you employed…"

_____

_____

_____

The 3 Categories of Presuppositional Forms

Existence - presupposing that something exists in the world

"Fred and **Sally** went to the **store."**
"Blue **wombats** are coming."

Time - *presupposing that something has happened, or will happen in the future*

*"Fred and Sally **went** to the store."*
*"Blue wombats are **coming."***

Quality - presupposing or assuming by emphasizing qualities in something

"Blue wombats are coming."

A Word about Practice

If you want, with practice you can easily learn all 22 presuppositional forms. Or, you can pick a few favorites to use from the ones you will be learning during the presentation in a training.

However you decide to do it!

Practice cards are available, and highly recommended! Very small to fit in any pocket. They also contain a "coding" that uses fonts and color to help you remember the categories. You can purchase them via the Expanding Enterprises, Inc. Web site.

It is not necessary to know the names of the forms from the field of linguistics. Just practice with a little guidance, and you will be amazed how quickly and easily your brain can learn to duplicate "types" of sentences.

But first, let's notice how easily we can plug target presuppositions into each of the following sentence forms.

On each of the following pages, you should write out your own presuppositions in the boxes below the examples. These pages are from a practice workbook used in an Expanding Enterprises, Inc. advanced training on Language Patterns.

The box on top is to write examples that presuppose the states you want to induce in your listener.

The center box is to write examples that presuppose the attitudes you want your listener to have.

The bottom box is to write examples that presuppose facts you want your listener to accept.

Presupposing Existence

You presuppose something exists by
referring to in as the subject of a sentence.
This can be further emphasized by the structure of
the sentence.

Relative Clauses

Stronger than "just a noun," to presuppose existence, is a noun followed by a phrase beginning with *who, which* or *that* –

"Of these performance objectives, which will help you improve the most?"
"It is your persistence that will most make this change."
"Your friends are people who will help you enjoy life more."

Cleft Sentences

Also stronger than "just a noun," is a sentence beginning with *It was/is* noun argument –

"It is clear performance objectives that help your performance improve."
"It is your creative part that will make this change for you."
"It is your mother who taught you ways to enjoy life more."

Negative Questions

You can also presuppose that something exists by <u>questioning</u> it NOT existing –

"<u>Haven't</u> you improved your performance during the past year?"
"<u>Don't you</u> know how smoothly people can change?"
"<u>Haven't you</u> begun to enjoy life more?"

Contrary-to-Expectation Should

Here is another way to presuppose that something exists by <u>questioning</u> it NOT existing –

"If you should happen to not improve your performance, then we will reorganize this."
"If you should happen to not make this change, then maybe I need to provide you with more information."
"In the unlikely event that you don't start enjoying life more, we will hunt you down and presuppose it more often."

Spurious Not

One more way to presuppose that something exists by
<u>questioning</u> it NOT existing –

"I wonder if you're not improving your performance already?"
"It appears you're not understanding how this might change."
"Should we try to get you to not enjoy life more?"

Qualifiers

Or, you can simply use the words, *"only, even, except, just, etc."* -

"Just the clarity of these objectives assures us your performance will quickly improve."
"Even having so many choices helps you change."
"Music isn't the only way to enjoy life more."

Presupposing with Time

In this use, the word "Time" has two meanings:

1. *That something either will happen in the future, or has happened in the past.*

2. *That this is not the first instance of something - not the first or only "time" it has happened.*

Counterfactual Conditional Clauses

Questioning if something didn't ALREADY happen —

"If your performance weren't improving, we wouldn't be here planning further improvement together!"
"If people weren't satisfied with my counseling, I wouldn't have so much repeat business."
"If you weren't learning to enjoy life more, you could start now."

Repetitive Verbs and Adverbs

Verbs and adverbs beginning with re - repeatedly, return, restore, retell, replace, renew —

"This opportunity can renew your history of steady improvement."
"Sometimes, you change the same problem repeatedly until the change is comfortable."
"You can learn to enjoy life repeatedly by practicing."

Repetitive Cue Words

Words that indicate repetition, such as too, also, either, again, back, etc. —

"Did you also find other areas where your performance is improving?"
"In addition to changing problems, we can also enhance resources."
"Are you going to practice enjoying life more at work too?"

Subordinate Clauses of Time

Words such as before, after, during, as since, when, prior, while, etc. —

"As your performance improves, we give you raises and promotions."
"While you are making changes, you need to remember the qualities you want to keep steady as well."
"After you practice enjoying life more, you'll understand why it's so important."

Change-of-Time Verbs and Adverbs

Words such as begin, start, stop, continue, proceed, already, yet, still, anymore, etc. —

"If you were looking for some way to start improving, this is it."
"Your innate kindness can help you continue to change."
"The sooner you begin enjoying life more, the sooner you will feel better."

Complex Adjectives

Words such as new, old, former, present, previous, etc. –

"By focusing your efforts in these key areas, you can get new levels of performance from your work."

"I don't know if you have had any previous stable changes."

"Are you at present aware of the benefits of enjoying your life more often?"

Ordinal Numbers

Describe this as the first, second, third, fourth, another, etc.-

"Another thing that will improve your performance is..."
"Will this be the first time you have confidently changed?"
"Is this the first or second time you've practiced the skills of enjoying life more?"

Presuppositions that use Qualities

By having the listener focus their attention on qualities and comparisons, the existence of the things named in the sentence is less likely to be questioned.

We can invite our listeners to compare qualities of things in many ways...

Change-of-State Verbs

We can use words like *change, transform, turn into, become,* etc. –

"The more you learn about this, the more your interest turns into excitement."
"This area of development can help you become a better performer at work."
"Carefully selecting the right change is what transforms it into a change you enjoy."

Factive Verbs and Adjectives

Words like *odd, aware, know, realize, regret* etc.

"You need to realize what an exciting opportunity this really is."
"When you know about the steps to improving your performance, you begin to understand how easy it can be."
"Most people are not aware of how comfortable a change can be."

Comparatives

Words like *more, less,* or words that end in *-er* –

"Do you know other employees who are improving their performance more than you are?"

"The quality of this change allows you to feel comfortable faster than with lesser changes."

"Some people find enjoying life much easier than others."

Comparative As

Or we can compare two things by using the sentence structure, *...as X as...* –

"Are you improving your performance as much as you need to for this promotion?"
"After a good counseling session, you should feel as changed as possible."
"Few lives offer as much opportunity for enjoyment as yours does."

Commentary Adjectives and Adverbs

Words like *luckily, fortunately, happily, cool, out-of-sight, innocently, necessarily... –*

"Luckily, your performance is improving."
"Fortunately you can also change smoothly and easily."
"Anchoring is a very cool way to begin enjoying your life more."

Pseudo-Cleft Sentences

Or we can make two statements about something in the form: What [sentence] is [sentence].

"What most helps people perform better is clear performance objectives."
"What this change can do is help you enjoy your life more."
"What enjoying your life more does best is improve your sense of satisfaction."

Rhetorical Questions

We can also ask "Rhetorical Questions" –

"What difference does it make if you aren't improving your performance a lot?"
"What good does it do to focus on how much you like this change?"
"Who cares if you enjoy life quickly?"

Questions

Questions, carefully formulated, are the most powerful form of presupposition!

"What part of this whole thing do you find most exciting?"
"How is this change better and different than any you've made before?"
"Which part of enjoying life more interests and excites you the most?"
"How quickly will you discover yourself using presuppositional forms all the time?"
"Did you think presuppositions were cool even before you started practicing?"

Emphasis and Voice Stress

Remember, by properly using emphasis and voice stress, you can make ANY presuppositional form more powerful!

"Perhaps it is improving PERFORMANCE that we most need to focus on here."
"Do you know of any other changes you've made with THIS kind of quality?"
"Do you think you will notice results QUICKLY?"
"You don't have to UNDERSTAND presuppositional forms to be able to use them effectively all the time."

A Little Test...

Below are pairs of sentences.
One of the sentences contains more presuppositional forms.
Circle the sentence that has more presuppositional forms present.

1.) a.) Was learning the basics of presuppositions easy?
    b.) Were other things that you have learned as easy as presuppositions?

2.) a.) It is practicing that makes you proficient at presuppositions.
    b.) Practicing will make you proficient at presupposing ideas.

3.) a.) Aren't you excited about using presuppositions?
    b.) Do you find presuppositions exciting?

4.) a.) You should be excited about what you can do with presuppositions.
    b.) If you should happen to not be excited about presuppositions, check your pulse.

5.) a.) Presuppositions have an impact on people.
    b.) Would someone go to all this trouble if presuppositions did not work?

6.) a.) Presuppositions are very powerful communication tools.
    b.) Using just a few presuppositions can be very powerful.

7.) a.) If you didn't learn presuppositions, this page would be impossible.
    b.) This page will help you learn presuppositions.

8.) a.) The more you use presuppositions the more you will learn about them.

b.) Using presuppositions repeatedly will help you develop skill.

9.) a.) Did you also find presuppositions easy to learn?

b.) Presuppositions are easy to learn.

10.) a.) Practicing presuppositions will help you to learn them.

b.) While you practice presuppositions, you will also be learning them.

11.) a.) You may start using presuppositions all the time without trying.

b.) You can use presuppositions all the time.

12.) a.) You will discover ways to use presuppositions with practice.

b.) The more you practice, the more new ways to use presuppositions you will discover.

13.) a.) I wonder what you will do the first time you notice you are using presuppositions?

b.) What will you do when you use presuppositions?

14.) a.) You can learn to use presuppositions constantly.

b.) You could easily become a person who uses presuppositions all the time.

15.) a.) When you realize how easy they are, you wonder how they can be powerful.

b.) Presuppositions are easy but powerful to use.

16.) a.) Some people use presuppositions more frequently than others.
b.) You can learn to use presuppositions often.

17.) a.) Did you think that presuppositions would be easy to learn?
b.) Are presuppositions as easy to use as you thought they would be?

18.) a.) Fortunately, you can always get better at using presuppositional forms.
b.) You can get better at using presuppositional forms.

19.) a.) Presuppositions can be powerful.
b.) What is most impressive is how powerful presuppositions can be.

20.) a.) You don't need to memorize all 22 forms to make presuppositions work.
b.) What difference does it make that you don't have all 22 forms memorized?

21.) a.) Have you already begun to plan broader areas of your life where you will utilize presuppositional forms?
b.) Have you thought about where you will use presuppositions?

A Little Answer Key –

1.)   B

2.)   A

3.)   A

4.)   B

5.)   B

6.)   B

7.)   A

8.)   B

9.)   A

10.)   B

11.)   A

12.)   B

13.)   A

14.)   B

15.)   A

16.)   A

17.)   B

18.)   A

19.)   B

20.)   B

21.)   A

Now that you have seen the entire set of Presuppositional Forms, you will need to practice them a great deal in order to make them natural tools in a conversation.

Go to www.expandingenterprises.com and order the two sets of practice cards – one for SOM, the other for Presuppositions. They are literally designed to be small enough to fit in your hand so people do not see them if you are using them to practice.

Most often, people discover two or three of these patterns that work well on themselves, and they begin to think those few are the most powerful language patterns. Each of these patterns appeals to different brains. Learn them all, and notice the shifts in non-verbal behavior when one of them works.

Wrapping It All Together

1. Begin by immediately matching the voice tone of their greeting or introduction.

2. Mirror visually observed behaviors, including muscle tensions and breathing pace.

3. Ask for immediate outcome, and presuppose you will get it for them.

4. Elicit outcome and meta-outcome. Memorize value/criteria words. Get evidence for at least two values/beliefs.

5. Check ecology of outcome in the context of the meta-outcome.

6. Ask for obstacles and difficulties. Use language to place difficulties and obstacles in the past, and put outcome and meta-outcome in the future.

7. Shift question focus on customer's expectations of the interactions with you as a manager or therapist. Begin to lead customer's state into amore positive state as they discuss their expectations of you. Use both language and state leading.

8. Utilize presuppositional forms to assure customer you will meet their evidence requirements, and/or will satisfy their outcomes.

9. Follow through on helping them make a change.

Remember to enjoy yourself, and to use this material on yourself as well!

Section 5: Beliefs That Could Change the World

Beliefs That Could Change the World

Please carefully note that I am not in any way saying anything about TRUTH. Truth and believing are two very different things. Truths are beliefs that people have that are simply facts in their world, and (they believe) nothing can change them. It has been said that truth is unchanging. If you have been alive more than 25 years, you have probably had your own truths change several times. We could define truths for our purposes as beliefs that people absolutely will NOT allow you to alter, and simultaneously beliefs they will dislike you for questioning or trying to change. In fact, the best definition I can come up with for truth is simply beliefs that people become extremely emotional about. But if truths are facts about the world, facts can be shared and explained to others, and people can be made to understand the truth of the facts without the need for anger, hostility, threats or demands. Facts can "stand on their own."

I suggest that in the interest of surviving as human beings, that we all come to an agreement that **the more emotional a person becomes about their beliefs, the less likely those beliefs are to be true, or based on facts.** I am voting for an approach of "pure reasoning" versus "emotional forcing." I fully understand that people get very emotional about their beliefs, but as a big group of beings living together on the planet, we cannot decide what is true and what is not true simply on the basis of who gets the most worked up, who gets the biggest gun, or who can "convert" the largest number of people to their way of thinking. If we look at history, this has gotten us into trouble many, many times. Instead, truth needs to be calmly presented to people, perhaps even presupposed to them. But the more emotional a person becomes about their beliefs, the more you should begin to doubt them.

The fact is we are all human and living here in a big, huge community called, "Planet Earth." We have been running enough experiments on people and rats and monkeys over the ages to learn some very significant ideas. Certain things help to keep order in societies and systems, and other things help to create destruction and disorder.

Three Beliefs that Could Destroy the World:

1.) "Some people are just 'better quality people' than others."

This is the basis of racism and sexism. We (that means ALL human beings) have much more in **common** than we have different about us. When we focus on how we are similar, we help to build rapport and understanding. We all have different abilities developed, different "strengths" and different weaknesses, but overall, we have a lot in common. We need to be proud of our uniqueness, celebrate how we have developed a particular skill or ability – but we need to stop quickly when we try to think that this makes us "better quality" in some way than another person or another group of people.

One way we build prejudice is by ascribing particular qualities to different races of people. I remember growing up in a city that had a huge Mexican population. (To this day my heart "warms" when I hear Spanish spoken in a Mexican accent, as it reminds me of home!) It was very common for me to hear the phrase, "Those lazy Mexicans…" As I got to know more and more of the Mexican people in my community, I discovered that most of them worked at LEAST two jobs, often lived crowded together to save money, and saved and saved all week so they could send their hard-earned money back to Mexico to support their families - and they were VERY thankful to have the chance to do that! I actually believed as a young child that the word lazy meant, "Works two jobs!" I kept thinking, "People seem angry about laziness. Why is it so bad to have two jobs?" (I.e. – I picked up on the emotional tag on the laziness belief, but didn't understand why having two jobs was bad.)

Whenever we decide one "group" or "type" of person is better than another, we are truly ignorant. Generalizations like that simply don't hold up in light of facts. One of the purposes of enforced integration is so that people have the opportunity to interact with others from different groups and races. Sooner or later, you will begin to discover that those "thems" are an awful lot like "us." In fact, as long as you keep your eyes and your heart open, you will begin to discover that people are very, very similar. We all have likes and dislikes, and we all have abilities and limitations. They run the entire gamut. If you allow yourself to interact with other people long enough, you find there is "one in every crowd," no matter what "group" that crowd is made up of. But that one jerk does not define a quality present in everyone in the group.

Furthermore, any time someone tells you "this group is better than that group," you can pretty much bet that they are a member of the "better" group! If they have to build themselves up by tearing someone else down, then their sense of, "I'm an okay person" is probably not strong enough to stand on its own. If they tell you they are better than some other group or type of person, you can most certainly bet they are not. But I don't recommend pointing this out to them.

If we absolutely have to have prejudice, then I want to build some new prejudices – positive prejudices! Let's try to find the **good** things that different cultures and people do, and be "positively prejudiced" instead of negatively. Which group feeds you the best and the most food? Which group loves their children more than any other? Which group is most tolerant of stupid ideas? Which group will help you no matter what the cost? Which group shares resources best? It is STILL prejudice, but at least it is a different flavor! (Non-bitter!)

2.) "You must believe what I believe in order for us to get along."

What people believe and how people behave are two different things. I may object completely to what another person believes, but as long as they don't hurt other people with their beliefs - don't lead others into creating more hate in the world - then I support them in having the freedom to think whatever they want to think. We need to stop trying to control people's beliefs, and focus on controls for harmful and damaging behaviors. It is pretty simple to decide on the most basic harmful and damaging behaviors. And this writing down of such guidelines has been going on since ancient cultures like the Sumerians.

3.) "My God is the REAL God, and if you don't believe me, God and I both hate you."

For myself, this is a classic example of what I call, "Silly Human Ignorant Thinking." (Makes for a nice acronym too!) Religion is supposed to be about LOVE – at least that is what I was taught and believed since I was a child. I could feel it in my church, I could feel it when we sang together, and I could feel it in my heart when I prayed. So I am quite sure, based on my own experience rather than any specific teaching or dogma. Unfortunately, as we have come through the ages, we have distorted religion into "Laws about what to hate." I like to think God really meant, "Laws about what you should avoid so you can survive together more easily."

I remember seeing in a magazine a protest group in Washington D.C. One of the protesters was holding up a sign that said, "GOD HATES _____!" (No need to fill in the blank!) I remember absolutely cracking up laughing, just totally roaring with laughter, and holding onto my rocking stomach because I couldn't believe that somebody could be so stupid as to believe that God would "hate" something or someone. Then I looked at my parents, and they were looking at me with the utmost seriousness. My father began to explain to me why he thought it was true. Even though I respected him as an authority and a wise man, I knew in the deepest part of my being that my God did not hate anything or anyone.

A recent book summarized it beautifully. Allegedly, God sarcastically said to someone, "Sure! I gave man free will, and I get pissed off when he actually USES it. Yeah, right!" That just plain doesn't make sense. I like to think of it this way – we are all God's children, and he decided not to put a fence in the back yard. So he lets us run all over the place and do anything we want. Some of us go racing like lemmings off of cliffs. Some of us smack the other kids in the yard. Some of us sit down, hold hands and work to make each other feel good and grow together. Either way, we are all his children.

Any parent who has a little bratty monster for a child will tell you; you gotta love the brats too! If that human parent can do that, don't you think God can too?

You can take anything in the world, and help make the world a better place by celebrating it, promoting it, loving it and working to share it with others. Even if it is a totally wacky idea, you still can do a minimum amount of damage if you stick with "promoting what you want" versus "destroying what you don't want."

If your religion brings you peace and joy and happiness, then let your whole life express peace and joy and happiness. Then people will come up to you and ask you why/how you are so happy, and you have the perfect opportunity to welcome them into your way of life or thinking. The biggest batch of opposition I have encountered in teaching belief work is from Christians who fear I will somehow destroy their truths – and they most often respond with hatred, threats and hostility. I have read the Bible cover-to-cover six times, and I don't remember reading that as a "recommended plan of Christian action" anywhere! And worse yet, they never even bother to ask me if I am a Christian in the first place!

George Carlin said it beautifully in his typical terse style: "Religion is like a lift in your shoes. It's okay if you want to wear lifts in YOUR shoes, but don't go nailing lifts onto the native's feet!"

And the bottom line is, even if you ARE right about your God being the only real God, I'll find out just a moment or two after I die anyway.

Three Beliefs that Could Save the World:
1.) "There is something good in every single person."

To which I like to add, "And something good in every married person as well." I add the word single to point out there are no exceptions. One of my most foundational beliefs (widest scope) is that there is something good in every person. My many years of experience in counseling and treating the criminally insane tested this belief to no end! However, there was always at least one redeeming quality - even in the worst criminals with whom I worked. Even if it was just that they loved one small child somewhere, or at the very least, that they could do good physical labor.

For the rest of my life, I will always remember being out in a locked and guarded courtyard with a team of mental health staff, supervising a basketball game that the patients were playing that was "getting out of hand." Here was a group of serial killers, rapists, thieves and torturers playing an absolutely VISCIOUS game of basketball. There were guys leaving the game bleeding, and some of the staff were discussing cutting the basketball game off – which was not going to be an easy thing to do! Suddenly, ALL of the players on the far north end of the basketball court (where the ball was being dribbled across some downed player's chest) began shouting, "WHOA!! HO! STOP!! HOLD IT!!!" The players all FROZE in position. A mother duck and her four chicks marched from their nest in the corner of the courtyard over to a large puddle at the other end of the courtyard, and for a brief moment, all of the playing stopped, all the violence stopped, and the baby ducks ran through this "corridor of violence." Everyone was laughing out loud, because the mother duck appeared to be yelling at everyone on either side as she led her kids through the mayhem. The game then resumed, almost – but not quite – as vicious as it had been a moment before! With all of our planning, prompting and hoping to get the players to calm down – it simply "happened" by the introduction of a bunch of baby ducks.

Everyone has something good about them or inside of them. Some people work very hard to keep it covered, but we need to trust it is there and work to "highlight" it in them. I discovered early on in working at that hospital that the most effective counselors had an "image" in their mind of the patient being more sane and better behaved than they currently were. Somehow, the patient always seemed to sense this high expectation, without it ever being verbally communicated. And they tried to live up to that expectation.

2.) "What I do, think and feel makes a difference in the world."

You can never know the full impact you have on your environment, but what you do makes a difference. If we each take more responsibility for our own behavior and the impact it has on others, we can make it through this world together. We can also learn how important it is to help others instead of throwing up barriers and difficulties for them.

I remember going to the grocery store one day, and I had been job hunting. I was horribly, horribly depressed. I felt like nobody wanted me. I was quickly running out of money, and I was having trouble concentrating. I even swallowed back tears as I went into the grocery store. I went to the grocery store just to get some food with the little money I had left. When I walked in, a young girl behind the service counter looked at me with a huge smile and said, "Hi! How are you today?" Her smile was so warm, so friendly, so inviting – not seductive or "forceful." Just a smile. I felt like a thousand pound weight was immediately lifted off of my chest. I smiled back at her and said, "I'm fine, how about you?" She grinned and said to me, "I'm fine. And thanks for the smile!" I kept grinning and said, "You probably recognize this smile – because I just caught it from you!" She laughed, and went about her work. I'm sure she was just "feeling friendly," but her smile stayed with me. In a single moment, she lifted a depression that had been building for weeks. I was amazed at the impact she had on me. And I'm sure she had no clue.

If you are feeling like the whole world is against you, and somebody politely lets you in his or her lane in traffic, it can change you. I am in total support of the "Random Acts of Kindness" campaign, because sometimes very simple acts of kindness can impact a person at a time when they are forming important beliefs, and it "flavors" or influences those beliefs in a positive way. You don't have to be "Mother Theresa" or be always kind to people in order to have a positive influence. The more people there are out there acting randomly kind, the more kindness there will be in the world. We can't just "hope" the world will change in some direction. We have to live the kind of life where what we want to find in the world around us comes out from ourselves! Only then can we expect it from other people.

3.) "Love and compassion are the most powerful and positive forces in the universe."

Whatever you love, love it deeply, dearly and intensely. Live your life as if you were always standing in the presence of someone or something you love. That will help you avoid acting in hateful ways. If you are wondering if you should do something or not do something, imagine later that day telling your children, your spouse, or even your "dream lover" about what you are doing and why you are doing it. If it involves a lengthy explanation of why you are doing it, you may want to think twice before acting.

It is one of my beliefs that our feelings and emotions have an actual "influence" on the world around us. I actually believe that if I feel loving feelings and stand next to a plant or another person, without saying or doing anything else, I am having a positive impact on them. I also believe that if I stay in a loving state inside myself, I am much more able to interconnect with people and more able to absorb and transmute some of the negative influences I encounter.

An Amazing Fact about Cooperation

There is a very interesting book called, "Games of Life" by Karl Sigmund. [Oxford University Press, Inc., New York NY, 1993] Sigmund is a mathematician, and the book is about applying the mathematics of game theory to ecology, evolution, relationships and other areas. In it he describes computer models of cooperation and competition. One of the most intriguing aspects of this book is that the amazing genius who wrote it has an excellent sense of humor. He makes jokes out of complicated mathematical discoveries.

I would love to devote pages to clarification, but the bottom line is – cooperation between parties to achieve goals is FAR more beneficial than the attitude or the behaviors of cheating or competition. Even if a person want to lie, cheat and steal their way through life, they may get some temporary benefit from these behaviors, but in the long run they would have fared much better with cooperative behaviors than their uncooperative behaviors.

Somehow, this fact has not soaked into the minds of people living in the 21st century. I believe it is beginning to seep through to many people, but is not yet all that mainstream. What is humorous about this is that the immense power of cooperation and pushing simultaneously in the same direction with united force so easily and clearly outweighs the benefits that cheating and not cooperating produces, that anybody who learns to understand the mathematics of that benefit would be quickly converted to cooperation. But at this point in time, many people think that "Joining hands to cooperate is a bunch of tree-hugging hippie crap! I have to FIGHT my way to the top! If you have something I want, I have the right to do ANYTHING I want to do to get it." While this has been an almost accepted way of thinking in our culture, the impact of such behaviors on the larger society is extremely damaging on all levels. Separation is not what we want to celebrate. Uniqueness is.

There is a project called, "The Venus Project." The people involved in this project have not just discovered the value of cooperation, but they are forming a sort of alternative culture and society in which cooperation is foundational. Several billionaires have been keeping their eye (and a lot of their money) on/in this organization, and I hope that their experiment is a tremendous success. Visit **www.thevenusproject.com** for more information.

Another guiding source of cooperative efforts is the United Nations' Sustainable Development Goals, which is collection of 17 global goals developed by leaders from 193 countries and organized by the United Nations in 2015. The categories of goals include things like No Poverty, End Hunger, Quality Education, Gender Equality, Clean Water and sanitation. You can download a copy of the document at:
www.un.org/sustainabledevelopment/sustainable-development-goals

I have my own project aimed at supporting the "Good Health and Well Being" category called, "The Tribe of Ninesm Project." It is my goal to teach 10,000 people my class I call, "The Shifting Memories Methodsm." I am disgusted that nobody has stepped up to support veterans and other people with Post-Traumatic Stress Disorder, and the medical insurance companies refuse to support non-medical treatment methods or reimburse therapists for working with anything less than the most severe PTSD cases. You can find out more about this project at www.expandingenterprises.com.

Section 6: Changing Generalizations About People and Groups

Changing Generalizations about People and Groups

Whenever you hear strong emotional negative beliefs about groups of people coming from someone, remember to stay calm, and comment on their emotional state, **not their belief**. You want to help people separate out their emotions from the belief. If their emotional state is extremely strong, just work to stay in a loving state within yourself. Sometimes the most powerful thing you can do is "stand in the face of hate" and just let it blow past you like wind. You don't have to do anything else. You do not have to have a good comeback, solve their problem, or otherwise change their hate. Sometimes, just letting them fester in their negative emotions makes them more aware of their emotions. Many people just like to be fired up emotionally about something. I believe this is the purpose of sports – to offer people a reason to scream and cheer and get excited, about an activity they are just observing passively! So for many people, talking about things that anger them is actually a very pleasant experience. Again, staying calm makes their extreme state a mismatch for your interaction, and by not following their lead, you are leading them back into a calmer state.

Next, you may want to discover their "meta-outcome." The meta-outcome is, "What they want behind what they want." For example, let's say a person has decided they hate Martians, and they want all the Martians out of the world. You simply ask them, "What's important to you about having all the Martians gone?" Or, you can ask, "What would having all the Martians gone do for you?" They might reply, "There would be fewer lazy people in the world." You then respond, "So what you really want is to have fewer lazy people in the world." You could even explore, "Well, how does Martian laziness impact you in YOUR world? Do you work with a lot of these lazy Martians? Is your daughter dating one? How is this a problem for you?" This is shrinking the frame from a generalization about "all Martians" to just the Martians in their world.

If you know them at all, you may know the location in which they store not-true beliefs, and you can repeat their belief back to them, while gesturing moving the belief toward the "not-true zone." You can also gently but carefully challenge their belief by using the sleight-of-mouth patterns listed in this book.

Another fabulously powerful way for people to overcome prejudice is to work with people of other cultures, races and groups on projects. When people work together as equals or peers on a common goal, the cooperative experiences they have during the interactions with the other people become examples for new generalizations about the members of that group. Even one living counter-example to a generalization begins to shift the extent of their "commitment" to particular prejudices about "those types of people."

And always remember, when we divide the world into "People we call Us" and "People we call Them," we are missing the bottom line. We are all people, with our own likes, dislikes, behaviors, qualities and lives. People have an amazing number of things in common, yet somehow we prefer to focus on what is "different." This emphasis tends to create separateness, and separateness is the Great Illusion. As the world becomes more and more interconnected, and because of our ability to communicate with each other, it is important that we develop skills and techniques that lead to better understanding and increased tolerance. That way, we can pool our resources, share our resources and thus make the world a better place for everyone on the planet.

Creating Positive People Beliefs

While it would be nice to have absolutely no prejudice in the world and have people just meet each other "being to being," this is a major change for the world to move toward, and I don't think we are quite there yet. I think it might be quite useful in the meantime to search for "positive prejudices." I would like different groups and cultures to "brag" about what they value most – what they would like to be "known for." Every culture has things they value that are slightly different than other cultures. Cultural groups should be able to proudly state what they want to be known for! That way, the "name" or label of a group would call-up images and ideas they want, in addition to (and maybe even instead of) other negative things with which they didn't want to be associated.

How to Teach and Practice Tolerance

There are two important distinctions people need to learn. The first is between feelings or attitudes, and behavior. When I worked with the criminally insane, some of the people had done things I believed were absolutely horrific! I absolutely hated what some of them had done. As a professional therapist, I had to keep my feelings about their past behavior to myself, and interact with them in the present, without much regard for what they had done in the past. Most of all, I had to search for and support any type of kindness, any type of "insight" into their own behavior, and any type of growth in their own ability to take responsibility. If I had my attention inside, I would "miss" those opportunities for growth. I may feel angry and resentful toward someone, but if I can maintain my behavior, I am helping the world be a more loving place by not expressing my negative feelings. This does not mean in any way that I deny the feelings – I feel them, I accept them and I acknowledge them. I just choose in that moment to very, very carefully monitor and control my behavior, to make sure it is not influenced by my internal state. In order to do that, I need to rely more on my thinking and less on my feelings. That way, I keep my feelings from taking control of my behavior. My feelings happen on the inside, and are my personal business. My behavior happens on the outside, and affects or influences everyone around me. I am hoping you have guessed that I could disassociate in order to lessen my intense feelings while I interact with the person.

The second thing we need to learn is that while they may feel absolutely certain that something is true, other people may not accept that truth. You may argue well, may be absolutely right, and may present a thousand reasons why another person should agree with you. If they do not, we need to learn to simply "drop it" and move on with our lives. Just because other people agree with you does not make you right. And just because other people disagree with you does not make you wrong. We need to learn to be comfortable in both of those situations. The American culture in which I live places such an incredibly high value on "the right answer," that we often shut out very good ideas and very correct ideas because they are not the "accepted" idea.

Section 7: Final Thoughts on How to Identify "Good" Beliefs

Final Thoughts on How to Identify "Good" Beliefs

1. Measure or evaluate beliefs with the rule: "If everyone believed this, would the world be a better place for all of us to live together, or a nastier place for some?"

2. You don't have to change major beliefs in order to get major changes. Sometimes you can make a little change, and the effect or impact ripples throughout the person's life. If you help a person believe, "I am a worthwhile person," you have had an incredible influence in their life.

3. You don't have to change a belief in order to change a person's relationship with the belief. Sometimes fighting with them about their belief simply makes them take that stand more strongly. If instead, you just listen to their belief with very little emotional reaction, you cause them to very deeply examine the belief. They may "put on a show" and have intense emotional reactions. But if you just stand in the face of that, you are forcing them to re-evaluate the belief.

4. Be cautious of believing "experts." I have worked with people who had very advanced degrees who were quite frankly, incredibly stupid. I have also met people who had 3rd or 4th grade educations who were incredible fountains of wisdom! Some of my most tangled problems were solved by Ellen, the lady who cuts my hair.

5. Be nice (or at least neutral) to people by default. It doesn't cost you anything. It at least reduces the likelihood that they will be nasty to you. And if they are carrying a gun and intending to just randomly shoot people, they just might exclude you.

6. Remember, you can use the patterns and questions and presuppositions in this book to change your own beliefs as well. If you want to claim you know how to do conversational hypnosis, then I expect that you would have installed at least 100 different hypnotic changes into yourself already.

7. Remember – to remember things for which you are grateful before you fall asleep each night. It really does work!